OURS BY RIGHT

WOMEN'S RIGHTS AS HUMAN RIGHTS

Edited by Joanna Kerr

(Zed)

ZED BOOKS *in association with*

THE NORTH-SOUTH INSTITUTE
L'INSTITUT NORD-SUD

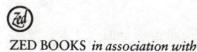

Ours by Right was first published by Zed Books Ltd,
57 Caledonian Road, London N1 9BU and 165
First Avenue, Atlantic Highlands, New Jersey
07716, USA in association with The North–South
Institute, Institut Nord–Sud, 200 – 55 Murray,
Ottawa, Canada K1N 5M3 in 1993.

Cover design by Andrew Corbett
Typeset by Opus 43, Cumbria, UK
Printed and bound in the United Kingdom
by Biddles Ltd, Guildford and King's Lynn.

A catalogue record for this book is available
from the the British Library
US cataloging-in-publication data is available
from the Library of Congress

ISBN 1 85649 227 3 Hb
ISBN 1 85649 228 1 Pb

The North–South Institute

The Institute is a Canadian non-profit corporation established in 1976
to provide professional, policy-relevant research on the 'North–South'
issues of relations between industrialized and developing countries. The
results of this research are made available to policy makers, interested
groups and the general public to help generate greater understanding and
informed discussion of development questions. The Institute is independent
and non-partisan, and cooperates with a wide range of Canadian,
overseas and international organizations working in related activities.

CONTENTS

FOREWORD

There is a growing conviction among women activists in virtually every country that women's rights are human rights. However, securing rights for women – rights within the family, rights to own property, rights to abortion, rights to vote, rights to move about freely without a husband's or male relative's agreement, rights to pass on citizenship – frequently have not been seen as central to 'development'. In countries of the North, the fight for legal rights has animated women's struggle for separate personhood, as legal rights have always been seen as stepping stones to (still elusive) equality. This struggle for just, legal treatment for women is now going on around the world.

There has been a peculiar myopia about women's rights in agencies which manage overseas development assistance. For about ten years, most aid agencies have had staff with particular responsibility for 'women in development' (WID). There have been 'gender training courses', special offices, special funds, and policies to 'integrate' women into development projects across the spectrum from civil aviation to agriculture. There has even been a change of rhetoric to include projects on 'women's empowerment'. In aid agencies, the WID staff – almost always women – are usually devoted, overworked and on the defensive. They must continually champion the utility of working on 'women and development'.

This book is based on the international conference 'Linking Hands for Changing Laws: Women's Rights as Human Rights Around the World'. The conference resulted from a discussion between myself and Rebecca Cook, the associate professor and director for the International Human Rights Programme at the University of Toronto's Faculty of Law. We felt very strongly that development agencies and donor institutions must catch up on the efforts of women in poor countries for legal equality. The conference brought together women who, through their scholarship and activism, are leading the fight in their countries for women's rights as human rights. Women and men from ministries of foreign affairs and aid agencies, and women from Canadian and American foundations, joined them for an exciting day and a half in Toronto. The conference provided an

opportunity to hear from women in the South. The resulting dialogue contributed to the international understanding and solidarity that is vital if the
world is to become more economically equitable and if women are to have
their rightful place within it.

Maureen O'Neil
President
The North–South Institute

ACKNOWLEDGEMENTS

First and foremost, I would like to thank the International Centre for Human Rights and Democratic Development (ICHRDD), which provided much of the funding for the international conference 'Linking Hands for Changing Law: Women's Rights as Human Rights Around the World' on which this book is based. ICHRDD also provided financial support to purchase forthcoming copies of this publication for delegates at the UN Conference on Human Rights in Geneva in June 1993.

The Canadian International Development Agency has also been generous, providing travel funds so that Southern participants could attend the 'Linking Hands' conference.

Thanks must also go to the Dutch Ministry of Foreign Affairs, which has paid for the publication of this book.

The conference was a major undertaking which could not have happened without the indispensable help of Fenella Porter, Ann Kerr, Lynne Hately and Juanita Montalvo. I would also mention the contribution of the North–South Institute's editorial team, Clyde Sanger, Rowena Beamish, Maureen Johnson and Lady Tinor in preparing the manuscript for Zed Books.

Joanna Kerr
The North–South Institute
Ottawa, Canada

Disclaimer

The presentations in this book are based on speeches given at the 'Linking Hands For Changing Laws' international conference on women's rights organized by the North–South Institute in Toronto, Canada, in September 1992. Opinions of the authors are their own and do not necessarily reflect those of the organizations for which they work.

GLOSSARY

CABW	Coordinated Action for Battered Women
CARICOM	Caribbean Community and Common Market
CECF-SP	Conselho Estadual da Condicao Feminina do Estado de Sao Paulo
CEDAW	Convention on the Elimination of all forms of Discrimination Against Women
CFEME	Centro Feminista de Estudos e Assessoria
CIDA	Canadian International Development Agency
CIM	Inter-American Commission of Women
CLADEM	Comite Latinoamericano para la Defensa dos Direitos da Mulher
CODESA	Conference on a Democratic South Africa
COSATU	Congress of South African Trade Unions
FIDA	Federation of Lawyers in Uganda
FLS	Forward-Looking Strategies
GAD	Gender and Development
GATT	General Agreement on Tariffs and Trade
ICT	Institute of Contextual Theology
ILO	International Labour Organization
IMF	International Monetary Fund
IWRAW	International Women's Rights Action Watch
LEAF	Women's Legal Education and Action Fund
NCW	National Coalition of Women
NGO	Non-Governmental Organization
OAS	Organization of American States
OECD	Organization for Economic Cooperation and Development
OECD/ DAC WID	OECD's Development Assistance Committee on Women in Development
PAC	Pan Africanist Congress
PRA	Participatory Rural Appraisals
SACC	South African Council of Churches
SADCC	Southern Africa Development and Coordination Conference
UNCED	United Nations Conference on Environment and Development
UNESCO	United Nations Educational, Scientific and Cultural Organization
UNFPA	United Nations Population Fund
UNHCR	United Nations High Commissioner for Refugees
UNICEF	United Nations Children's Fund
UNIFEM	United Nations Fund for Women
WHO	World Health Organization
WID	Women in Development
WiLDAF	Women in Law and Development in Africa
WLSA	Women and Law in Southern Africa
WLUML	Women Living Under Muslim Laws

ABOUT THE
CONTRIBUTORS

BARBARA ADAMS is a senior programme officer at the UN Non-Governmental Liaison Service in New York. She was previously associate director of the Quaker United Nations Office, and has worked as a consultant for UNICEF. She was an official observer at the 1985 Nairobi Conference of the UN Decade for Women.

GEORGINA ASHWORTH is founding director of CHANGE, launched in 1979 to do research and publish reports on the status of women internationally. She was research director of the Minority Rights Group, London, 1974–79 and Visiting Fellow at the Institute of Education, University of London 1986–89. Her most recent publication is as editor of *A Diplomacy of the Oppressed: Directions in International Feminism* (Zed Books 1993).

THE HON. EDWARD BROADBENT is president of the International Centre for Human Rights and Democratic Development in Montreal. From 1975 until 1989 he was federal leader of Canada's New Democratic Party. In 1978 he was elected vice-president of Socialist International, and was particularly involved in efforts to bring peace to Central America. Before entering active politics, he was Professor of Political Science at York University, Toronto.

CHARLOTTE BUNCH, feminist author, organizer, teacher and activist, has been a leading figure in the women's movement for over two decades. Her writings have appeared widely, and she has edited seven anthologies. She recently authored *Women's Rights as Human Rights: Towards a Revision of Human Rights*. She formerly held the Chair in Women's Studies at Douglass College, Rutgers University, New Jersey, and is currently professor in the School of Planning and Development and director of the Center for Women's Global Leadership at Rutgers.

FLORENCE BUTEGWA is the Uganda-born coordinator of the regional network of Women in Law and Development in Africa (WiLDAF), based in Zimbabwe. She is an active member of the Federation of Lawyers in

Uganda (FIDA) and the author of *Challenges of Promoting Legal Literacy among Women in Uganda*.

REBECCA COOK is director of the International Human Rights Programme in the Faculty of Law, University of Toronto, where she is an associate professor. She is also associate professor in the Faculty of Medicine's Department of Health Administration and has published many articles on health law, international human rights, abortion and sex discrimination.

ANDRÉE COTÉ practised family law and social law in Montreal after being called to the Bar in 1984. She has taught courses on Women and Law, and Law and Sexuality, at l'Université du Québec à Montréal, and was director of Canada's Court Challenges Programme, based on the Canadian Charter of Rights and Freedoms, until it was wound up under the 1992 federal budget.

SHANTHI DAIRIAM has, for 17 years, been an activist working for women's organizations in Malaysia, particularly in the areas of violence against women and reproductive rights, with the object of inserting gender concerns into the mainstream of national planning. She has also worked with the Asia–Pacific Forum on Women, Law and Development.

SÉNY DIAGNE is a lawyer in Senegal. She has been deeply involved in the setting up and operation of a legal aid clinic in Dakar, and has been concerned with women's rights. She is a member of Women in Law and Development in Africa.

MARY EBERTS is a founder of the Women's Legal Education and Action Fund (LEAF), which handles test case litigation under the Canadian Charter of Rights and Freedoms on behalf of women's equality rights. She has appeared as counsel in a number of women's equality cases before the Supreme Court of Canada and provincial Courts of Appeal, most recently acting on behalf of the Native Women's Association of Canada to assert, under the Charter, a right to participate in the 1992 constitutional talks. She is a partner in a Toronto law firm, teaches constitutional litigation at the University of Toronto, and has served on the Board of the Metro Toronto Action Committee on Public Violence against Women and Children.

ARVONNE FRASER is the director of the International Women's Rights Action Watch in the United States. She is a Senior Fellow at the Humphrey Institute for Public Affairs at the University of Minnesota. She was the first coordinator of the Women in Development Programme at the US Agency for International Development (USAID). She recently headed the US delegation to the UN Commission on the Status of Women.

MARSHA FREEMAN is deputy director of the International Women's Rights Action Watch in the United States, which monitors the implementation of the UN Convention on the Elimination of All Discrimination Against Women (CEDAW). She is former president of Minnesota Women Lawyers and reporter for the Minnesota Committee on Gender Fairness in the Courts, and is a Senior Fellow at the Humphrey Institute of Public Affairs at the University of Minnesota.

CAROLYN HANNAN-ANDERSSON is the acting head of the Gender Office in SIDA (Swedish International Development Authority). She has worked for over ten years in the field of Gender and Development, doing field research and project consultancies before becoming a full-time member of the SIDA gender programme. She worked for many years in Tanzania.

MARIE-AIMÉE HÉLIE-LUCAS is the Algerian-born international coordinator of the Women Living Under Muslim Laws Network. The network is compiling and comparing versions of Muslim law enacted as family codes in some 50 countries to determine whether these are religiously or culturally inspired.

JOANNA KERR is a researcher at the North–South Institute, Ottawa, coordinator of the 'Linking Hands' conference in Toronto in September 1992, and editor of this book. She has an M.A. degree in Gender and Development from the Institute of Development Studies at the University of Sussex. Her current research focuses on women's legal rights, violence against women and the effects of macroeconomic policies on women.

KAREN KNOP is a special lecturer in the Faculty of Law, University of Toronto, and is preparing a dissertation examining the interaction of feminism and sovereignty. In 1988–89 she studied in the Faculty of Law at Moscow University, and went on to specialize in public international law and Soviet international law at Columbia University, New York.

BRIGITTE MABANDLA is a legal adviser to the African National Congress at the Conference on a Democratic South Africa (CODESA). Detained for five months in 1974 for student activism, she spent the next 15 years in exile, gaining her LLB degree at the University of Zambia. She is coordinator of research on the constitutional rights of women and children at the Community Law Centre, University of the Western Cape. She is also coordinating a review of the African Charter for the Protection of Human Rights.

ELIZABETH MCALLISTER is director-general of the Americas Branch in the

Canadian International Development Agency (CIDA). In the last decade, she has been director of CIDA's Women in Development Directorate, during which she chaired the OECD-DAC Expert Group on Women in Development, counsellor (Development) in the Canadian Embassy in Indonesia, and director of CIDA's China Programme.

CECILIA MEDINA is Professor of International Human Rights Law in the Law Faculty of the Universidad Diego Portales in Santiago, Chile. She has a doctorate in law from the University of Utrecht, The Netherlands, where in the 1980s she taught human rights and international economic organizations. In 1990 and 1991 she organized and taught training courses for judges and lawyers in South America on international human rights law.

RASHIDA PATEL is a member of the Pakistan Women's Lawyers Association and has argued cases before the High Courts and the Supreme Court of Pakistan. She is the author of *Pakistan: Muslim Women and the Law*. She is also President of the All Pakistan Women's Association.

SILVIA PIMENTEL is Professor of Law at the Catholic University in Sao Paulo. She is the author of books on women's rights and was a prominent lobbyist for the inclusion of women's rights in the present constitution of Brazil. She is a member of the Board of Directors of International Women's Rights Action Watch and a member of the Latin American Committee for the Defence of Women's Rights (CLADEM).

LINDA POOLE has, since 1986, been the executive secretary of the Inter-American Commission on Women, a specialized agency of the Organization of American States in Washington D.C.; she has been an officer with the OAS for 21 years. Through her work, she has provided technical aid to member countries in institution building and the development of advocacy programmes on behalf of women.

DOROTHY Q. THOMAS is director of the Women's Rights Project (a component of Human Rights Watch U.S.A.) which monitors violence against women and sex discrimination worldwide. In 1989 she worked in Namibia with the Lawyers' Committee for Civil Rights Under Law, monitoring the transition from South African rule to independence and democracy.

PART I
Setting the Agenda

1

The Context and the Goal

JOANNA KERR

'Women's rights are human rights' is a proclamation for justice.

Women have the right to food, shelter, property, reproductive choice, social security, health care and employment. Women have the right to political and religious freedom of expression, freedom from torture or slavery, access to education, and the civil privileges of citizens. Women have the right to a livelihood free from all forms of violence.

These are their inherent rights. Yet they are being denied. So pervasive and systemic are the human rights abuses against women that they are regarded as part of the natural order.

As UNICEF has pointed out, the enjoyment of human rights and fundamental freedoms is 'likely to depend on the one cruel chromosome'.[1] In countries where a 'son-preference' is associated with economic survival, intentional neglect of daughters and female malnutrition are commonplace. This quote from a Bangladeshi woman is a disturbing illustration:

> How can you explain to children there is not enough food. When my son cries, I try to feed him. It is easier to make my daughter understand. . . . If there is less, we eat less. You have to feed men more, or they beat you. My son beats me if there is not enough food.[2]

In fact, according to one estimate, 100 million women are not alive today as a result of male-preference and female infanticide.[3]

For millions of women around the world, land ownership and access to credit are keys to survival, yet rarely their right. Current economic conditions and structural adjustment policies further deny women economic opportunity in every part of the world, without exception. Afshar and Dennis argue that:

> Changes in levels and composition of public expenditure have had an adverse impact on women both as consumers of welfare and public sector services and as its providers and employees. Furthermore, the adjustment policies tend to reallocate public resources towards repayment of loans, rather than provision of basic needs.[4]

In only a few countries do women have the freedom to choose the number of or spacing between children as government policy or social standards maintain authority over their bodies. In Brazil, for example, 7.5 million women of reproductive age are sterilized;[5] in Ireland, sharing information on abortion is illegal; and in China, state law prohibits women from having more than one child.

Women remain invisible victims of political oppression and are inherently forgotten as political actors. They are routinely sexually abused as prisoners, imprisoned for peaceful beliefs and activities, tortured, denied the right to a fair trial, abducted, 'disappeared', and extra-judicially executed.[6] These violations, assumed to be perpetrated only against men, prompted the 1992 Amnesty International special report on human rights abuses against women, which was long overdue. Women have yet to be safeguarded by the influence of international outrage and pressure.

Violence against women is the most pervasive abuse of human rights. It exists in various forms in everyday life in all societies. In Mexico, a woman is raped every nine minutes. An estimated 1,000 women are burned alive each year in dowry-related incidents in the state of Gujarat alone, in India. One in ten Canadian women are abused or battered by their husbands or partners.[7] The world must recognize that the protection of women's bodies and identities is not a privilege, but a right.

The Traditional Human Rights Framework

The magnitude of women's human rights abuses demands international action. There are universally agreed human rights laws and conventions, such as the Universal Declaration of Human Rights, which guarantee rights and freedoms to all people. They create the frame of reference for citizens within their national contexts to make claims for their rights. According to Charlotte Bunch, 'the notion of human rights is one of the few moral visions ascribed to internationally and is one of the few concepts that speaks to the need for transnational activism and concern about the lives for people globally.'[8]

This framework of rights promotion, however, does not ensure the rights of women. The ideals and philosophy of the Universal Declaration of Human Rights, adopted by the UN in 1948, is intended to protect the rights of men, women and children around the world. Within this instrument, human rights are defined broadly – 'where no distinction should be made on the basis of race, colour, sex, language, religion, political or other opinion, national or social origin, property, birth, or other status.' 'Non-discrimination on the basis of sex' does not eradicate gender inequality, however, because of the way in which this convention is interpreted and implemented.

The Declaration on Human Rights has created a hierarchy of rights, putting a priority on civil and political rights. These are assumed to be easily defined by law, recognized by consensus internationally and monitored by the UN Human Rights Commission. This has left the responsibility and protection of social and economic rights – reduced to a notion of basic needs – to national governments and international development agencies, with no binding guarantee that these rights exist. Civil and political rights are viewed therefore as inherent, universal and justifiable, while social and economic rights are viewed as evolving gradually as a matter of social policy rather than fundamental justice. Since universal gender inequality creates for women conditions of exploitation or subordination in the economic and social sphere, the lack of attention to these rights is of greater concern to women.

In addition, human rights declarations are universally recognized as contracts between the state and its peoples. As Georgina Ashworth notes, women are consequently neglected as their relationship with the state remains mediated by men, be they husbands, fathers, brothers or sons 'who at the same time acquire their authority over women from the state or traditional political community.'[9]

Similarly, the 1951 UN Geneva Convention on Refugees is a human rights instrument which discriminates against women. Persecuted women and girls who step out of their strict social roles are not offered sanctuary as refugees because gender is not a criterion to gain refugee status. Take the example of an Iranian woman who fled to Canada as a refugee after being given 35 lashes and being fired from her job for not wearing a veil within the privacy of her own home. She faced further prosecution in Iran for the offence, yet the Canadian government, in a May 1990 decision, did not recognize her as a refugee under the UN definition. She was sent back to Iran because, according to the Refugee Hearing Board, she risked only prosecution, not persecution; in addition, the Board said her punishment did not leave permanent injuries and the loss of her job did not deprive her of her livelihood.[10]

One human rights instrument, the United Nations Convention on the Elimination of All Forms of Discrimination against Women (CEDAW), is explicitly intended to secure rights for women. Adopted in 1979 by the UN General Assembly, it specifically acknowledges the extensive discrimination against women that continues to exist. The Convention emphasizes that such discrimination violates the principles of equality of rights and respect for human dignity. Altogether, it provides a comprehensive framework for challenging the various forces that have created and maintained discrimination based on sex.

Despite the value and merit of the CEDAW convention and its ratification by 119 governments, it has received little active support. State parties have lodged 80 substantive reservations to it – the highest number for any international convention. Meanwhile, unlike its affiliate, the Human Rights Committee, the CEDAW monitoring committee lacks the staff and money required to complete its work and the authority to investigate individual or group claims violations.

Instead of having high priority at the United Nations, women's human rights are given little attention; 'women's issues' are marginalized into under-funded and ineffective machineries. As a result, women around the world are demanding an extensive transformation of the existing deficient human rights framework. The perpetuation of the violation of women's human rights has also provoked women internationally to challenge the forces that obstruct their inherent rights – be they national governments, religion, culture, legal systems, international institutions or their own families. Women globally are demanding that their rights move beyond promises, into guarantees.

The Promotion of Women's Rights as Human Rights

A huge task is at hand. In order to ensure that women enjoy human rights and freedoms, policy makers must be lobbied, systems must be changed and attitudes must evolve. Reforms therefore are being urged at four levels: international mechanisms, national laws and policies, legal systems and, finally, the cultural norms of society.

At the international level, clearly the failure of the human rights mechanisms must be addressed. This entails the acknowledgement of women's rights as central to democracy and development within the predominantly male United Nations. The corollary is a Human Rights Committee that monitors the abuses of women's human rights in all their forms and a CEDAW which is adhered to by state parties.

Reform at the national level is about making governments – their laws, policies and actions – accountable to women. Undeniably, this is a great challenge. Creating the laws that ensure the rights of women is a first and fundamental step. Note, for example, the benefits of primary education, age of majority, voting rights, or maternity leave that women in many countries enjoy. However, as has been pointed out, in many parts of the developing world, the ideology of liberal individualism and rights is so removed from the reality of the vast majority of women's lives that the effect of resorting to rights and law is demobilizing rather than mobilizing for these women. Nonetheless, according to Marsha Freeman, 'unless we attempt to address the inequities in the current systems, we abandon them to those for whom gender equity is not a priority, leaving our legal fate in their hands.'[11]

Many feminist lawyers are challenging the male-centred construction of laws. It is also essential to introduce strategies which close the gap between the formal legal rights of women and their rights in practice. To make the existing legal and political institutions (the courts, the police and other areas of the justice system) work for women, they must be reformed.

Laws and institutions can be changed, yet without the transformation of values in society – be they cultural, religious, political or economic – which are destructive to women, few gains can be made. This transformation remains perhaps the greatest hurdle. According to Sri Lankan lawyer Radhika Coomaraswamy,

> in many ways, the issues of women's rights have accentuated the constant tension between tradition and modernity. Women have been classically regarded as the bearers of tradition from one generation to another. The transformation of their role in society is seen as an erosion of the foundation of traditional cultures.[12]

Similarly, governments consider male-biased relations of gender as being within the delicate realms of culture and the private sphere, beyond their jurisdiction. This, however, is a hypocritical stance, considering that taxation, social security, immigration, employment regulations, as well as marriage and family law, are all monitored by the nation-state and fall within the parameters of the private sphere.[13]

The Role of Development and Funding Agencies

This book is based on presentations at a conference entitled 'Linking Hands for Changing Laws – Women's Rights as Human Rights Around the World' held in Toronto, Canada, in September 1992. This meeting assembled international women's rights activists, legal scholars, government officials and representatives from bilateral and multilateral donor agencies, development institutions, foreign ministries and private foundations. A central objective was to consider the essential role that funding agencies play in women's rights promotion.

This consideration is particularly cogent considering the new focus on human rights. Democratization movements around the world and foreign policy shifts that reflect the emergence of environmental and social considerations are noteworthy developments that have created the conditions for the prevailing focus on human rights. 'Western' governments are now advocating democracy to nations that are reforming to multi-party states. Most development agencies have implemented human rights programmes and, more recently, programmes to support 'democratization and good governance'. Linkages are being made between human rights, development, democracy and sustainability. Also noteworthy is the increased dialogue on violence against women within the United Nations and the Organization of American States.[14]

This trend is encouraging but not yet worthy of commendation. Firstly, there is substantive literature which documents how the decision-making powers within development agencies continue to remain not only male-dominated but also gender-blind in orientation. It has taken considerable action by the international women's movement to get women's concerns even superficially integrated into development policy. Moreover, there is significant debate surrounding the definition or criteria of democracy. As some have argued, if democracy includes a notion of political representation, no government in the world is democratic as far as women are concerned (women are rarely represented by elected leaders).

Currently, women's rights are not implicitly part of human rights and good governance programmes within development agencies. Realignment of donor agency and government policies toward the inclusion of women's human rights into central policy and planning is paramount.

The Goal

The first part of this book establishes the challenge of women's human rights promotion around the world by two distinguished Canadian human rights activists.

From Pakistan to South Africa, from Brazil to Canada, the country experiences as described by prominent women's rights activists in Part II, highlight the intricacies of the struggles, accomplishments and setbacks in achieving women's human rights. Despite the very different national contexts, the experiences are ominously similar.

In the part entitled 'Mechanisms for Change', experienced authors from human rights law, development agencies, human rights organizations and women's groups explore the efficacy of approaches or mechanisms currently used to advance the rights of women – from the CEDAW monitoring and development policies to consciousness-raising among grassroots women. Information-packed chapters provide innovative methods to consider, as well as identifying prospective impediments to women's struggles.

In the final part, 'Strategies and Action', internationally renowned feminists present their astute perspectives on strategic areas of action to be targeted by women and donor agencies. The concluding chapter synthesizes the provocative debates that occurred at the Linking Hands conference and attempts to portray the wit, wisdom and tenor of the remarkable participants.

We hope that this book will be used by women and men as a basis for discussion and action in analysing the complexities of achieving women's human rights. We also hope that the book will be read by those policy makers who today are unaware of the mechanisms which perpetuate women's oppression so that they too, in their various capacities, will actively ensure the rights now denied to half of humanity.

NOTES

1 UNICEF (1992), *State of the World's Children*.

2 Naila Kabeer (1989), 'Monitoring Poverty as if Gender Mattered: a Methodology for Rural Bangladesh', Institute of Development Studies, Discussion Paper 255, February 1989.

3 Amartya Sen (1990), 'More than 100 Million Women are Missing', in *New York Review of Books*, Vol. 37, No. 20, 20 December, 1990.

4 Haleh Afshar and Carolyne Dennis, (eds) (1992), *Women and Adjustment Policies in the Third World*, Macmillan Press, p. 4.

5 Sylvia Pimentel, Chapter 5 below.

6 Amnesty International (1992), *Women in the Front Line: Human Rights Violations Against Women*.

7 These statistics are taken from MATCH International Centre (1990), *Linking Women's Global Struggles to End Violence*.

8 Charlotte Bunch (1991), 'Toward a Revision of Human Rights', in *Gender Violence: A Development and Human Rights Issue*, Center for Women's Global Leadership, Working Paper No. 1.

9 Georgina Ashworth (1992), 'Women and Human Rights', a background paper prepared for DAC Expert Group on Women in Development, Organization for Economic Cooperation and Development.

10 From Immigration and Refugee Board of Canada files.

11 Marsha Freeman (1991), 'Women's Human Rights and Reproductive Rights: Status, Capacity and Choice', in *Inter-American Parliamentary Group on Population and Development Bulletin*, Vol. 8, No. 9, October 1991.

12 R. Coomaraswamy (1982), 'A Third World View of Human Rights', in *UNESCO Courier*, No. 49.

13 Ashworth, 'Women and Human Rights'.

14 See chapters by Rebecca Cook, Linda Poole and Marsha Freeman for an account of recent advances.

2

Getting Rid of Male Bias

EDWARD BROADBENT

It is a sad truth that people who would never scoff at or belittle human rights do not treat women's rights with the same seriousness. In 1992 a woman from Saudi Arabia landed at Mirabel Airport, in Quebec, and asked for refugee status saying she was persecuted in her country as a woman who refused to accept second-class status. She had been stoned for revealing her hair. She reported that she was laughed at by immigration officials who dismissed such claims as cause for refugee status.

In addition to the violations of human rights that we readily condemn, women face a series of abuses that are normally ignored, overlooked and forgotten by the human rights community: forced childbirth, sexual slavery, rape, genital mutilation, discrimination in education and employment, female infanticide, domestic violence, sexual harassment. This depressing and only partial list describes a global phenomenon which has reached epidemic proportions.

The truth is that the international community has done precious little to correct these abuses. We have yet to see effective mobilization of international public opinion against states enacting discriminatory laws and repressing activists for women's rights. While cultural relativism and the principle of state sovereignty are no longer acceptable justifications for extra-judicial killings or torture, they are still being used as lame excuses to prevent the international community from speaking out on behalf of women whose fundamental human rights are denied in law and in practice.

There are at least some signs of change. Human rights organizations around the world are beginning to recognize that they cannot ignore 52 per cent of the population. Getting rid of that male bias means looking at human rights from a perspective that can account for both the female and male experience. I do not know whether it means re-writing the Universal Declaration of Human Rights, but it certainly means re-reading it. On one level, the increasingly popular slogan 'Women's rights are human rights' is simply stating the obvious. Yet it requires a concerted effort, both political and intellectual, to make this statement a reality.

'Women's rights are human rights' suggests a profound change in the way most people see international human rights. It means that, just as I have the right to 'life, liberty and security of the person', so do all women have the right to be free from violence in the street and the home, because that is what life, liberty and security means from a woman's point of view. It means that, just as I have the right not to be subjected to cruel, inhuman or degrading treatment, so should women be freed from forced childbirth, forced prostitution, clandestine abortions and genital mutilation – all of which are cruel, inhuman and degrading. It means that, just as I have the right to an education, so do the women who live in rural Nepal; yet only two per cent of them are functionally literate. The right to equality before the law means that, as human rights advocates, we must stand up not simply for the rule of law but simultaneously against all laws which discriminate against women.

The world will not change just because we put new lenses in our glasses. It will only change if we act and if we are given the means to act. As the President of the International Centre for Human Rights and Democratic Development, a body that is accountable to the Parliament of Canada, I take the funds at our disposal – limited as they are – as a most serious matter. A good portion of that money goes to the protection and promotion of women's rights, to the growing number of groups in all areas of the world that are fighting the poverty and disenfranchisement of women, and the violence against them. These groups often face tremendous hostility from their governments, and from the male-dominated societies in which they live. They require our solidarity, our collaboration and, last but not least, our financial support.

The International Centre will be funding women's groups to attend the regional preparatory meetings to the 1993 World Conference On Human Rights. Governments must be made to understand that human rights include women's rights and that any international forum that claims to discuss human rights must look at the situation of women and the specific abuses they confront. Women need to meet among themselves to determine priorities and strategies for change. The Convention on the Elimination of All Forms of Discrimination Against Women has now been signed by 119 countries, but not a single one of them has accomplished its paramount objective and raison d'être: the elimination of all forms of discrimination against women. There is a great deal of work to be done.

I urge other foundations and donors to support the women who are fighting to get their concerns on the agenda of the World Conference on Human Rights. We cannot condemn states which torture political prisoners without condemning those who condone domestic violence by failing to prosecute offenders. We cannot decry those states which forbid citizens their freedom of movement without decrying those states who refuse passports to women, prohibit women from driving, or prevent them from obtaining a legal medical procedure in a neighbouring country. We cannot claim to defend the international human rights treaties, if we do not examine them clause by clause and see what each means for women.

The language of human rights is powerful. It carries great moral authority, and is having an increasing impact on the peoples and the states of the world. If it is, however, to aspire to true universality, it must deal not only with the different experiences and realities of North and South, East and West, but also the different experiences of women and men. We must make the language of human rights relevant to women's lives.

3

Gaining Redress
Within a Human Rights Framework

REBECCA COOK

These reflections on the consultation on women's international human rights[1] held in Toronto in September 1992 are my own observations, and do not necessarily represent any kind of consensus. The goals of the meeting were to foster new dialogues between legal theorists and legal practitioners, and to advance more effective legal protection of women's human rights; to foster dialogue between advocates who work domestically and those who work internationally; and, finally, to foster dialogue between advocates working within women's NGOs and those working within the mainstream human rights NGOs.

We were trying to apply new theories of feminist analysis to problems that women face and to provide some redress within the human rights framework. (Indeed, there were questions about the validity of the human rights framework itself.) I will give three examples: the first is domestic violence against women; the second is the subordination of women by religious and customary laws; and the third is the structural adjustment issue in aid policies.

Domestic Violence against Women

The public–private distinction underlies many problems in trying to apply the human rights model to domestic violence. The law just does not reach to the private sphere of the family. More importantly, public international law, the state sovereignty model, does not necessarily reach to the private domain of the state. However, domestic violence is pervasive and structural. In international human rights terms, it is systematic and egregious; but it is not accommodated within the international human rights model. We tried to draw the analogy with torture or slavery and to see whether the convention against torture might be applied more effectively to deal with this problem. There was, as well, a great debate on whether citing the principle of unequal protection of the law was an effective and appropriate method to deal with domestic violence.

Subordination of Women by Religious Doctrines and Traditions

In some societies women cannot even leave their own home or their own country without the permission of their husbands. In other words, the protective and paternalistic model has turned women into property. We thought that one way forward was to work within the religious paradigm to develop female interpretations to free women from religious subordination. Another way was to use international human rights law to interpret religious law. We struggled with how we might use feminist theories to interpret religious law more creatively.

Structural Adjustment

We heard from several women about the devastating impact of structural adjustment on women and how these policies had marginalized them even further. The human rights model might help to show the injustice of structural adjustment.

Turning from financial policies to aid policies, these provide millions for agricultural development. But have agricultural agencies such as the International Fund for Agricultural Development really looked at the impact of their aid policies on women? Millions of women, in fact, just do not benefit from agricultural aid policies because in many parts of the world they cannot own or inherit land.

Some Personal Comments

One lesson I learned from the consultation as a northern feminist was how provincial I really am, and how important it is that a dialogue with southern feminists really happens. It is important in order to ensure that we are not divided as women – north and south, east and west – and that northern feminists are not missionary feminists but really global feminists who are listening and developing practical theories so that human rights really will benefit all women. It is important so that we can understand how our aid and financial policies continue to subordinate women, how we can advocate change in our own law schools and in our own communities, and, as global feminists, how we can empower women around the world to negotiate for their rights.

Among specific challenges that confront us in a very real way are the United Nations conferences during the next few years. For the 1993 Human Rights Conference we need to think very carefully about how we can best apply human rights to protect women in every community. The Convention on the Elimination of All Forms of Discrimination Against Women (CEDAW) and other human rights treaties can be used to do this. For the 1994 World Population Conference we need to figure out how the CEDAW, and particularly the sections in it dealing with reproductive rights, can be used to ensure that the conference is not yet another population conference that controls women's bodies in the interests of governments' own particular population policies. Again in 1994, the International Year of the Family, how can we use the CEDAW and other international human rights treaties to underscore the crucial point that governments have an obligation to eliminate private discrimination in the family and to ensure that the occasion is not used once again to compromise women's position in the family?

Finally, the 1995 UN Conference on Women in Beijing: is it going to be used as a means to rubber-stamp China's violations of human rights policies? How can we show that, in the same year that the Chinese government secured this conference for Beijing, they killed the important proposal, on which many feminists had worked, for a UN Special Rapporteur on violence against women. The appointment of a Special Rapporteur would have been one of the most effective ways of exposing violence against women. This is hardball politics, and we've got to learn how to play.

NOTE

1   These comments refer to presentations and discussions at a three-day consultation on women's international rights held prior to the international conference 'Linking Hands for Changing Laws' in Toronto. A full report on the consultation will be published in *Human Rights Quarterly*, Vol. 15, No. 2, 1993. Papers from the consultation will eventually be published in a book edited by Rebecca Cook entitled *Women's International Human Rights Law*.

PART II
Women's Rights –
Country Experiences

4

Change in South Africa – Advances for Women?

BRIGITTE MABANDLA

Two years ago, the people of South Africa began a process of negotiations for a democratic dispensation. However, on 16–17 May 1992, we experienced an impasse at the second plenary session of the Convention for a Democratic South Africa (CODESA). Many people believe that this was actually the period when we began negotiating a new constitution. This is not true; we were only at the preliminary stage of discussions on constitutional principles. Notwithstanding the impasse, the process of designing CODESA has had significant implications for women.

Even before the formation of CODESA, there were numerous meetings to prepare for the establishment of the negotiations forum. Talks went on at various levels and, in all these forums, women were excluded. There were also talks to curb the violence that was becoming very serious in the country, and again women were not involved in these structures. Yet on the ground women were continuously protesting, marching and consulting, and doing door-to-door campaigns against violence. The exclusion of women raised concerns among the women of South Africa; and the ANC Women's League spearheaded the process of networking among women around the issue of women's participation in the negotiations. In other words, it was the exclusion of women that inspired women to come together.

Workshops organized by the Women's League to network for the participation of women in the constitution-making process laid the foundation for women's collaboration during this period. This had a very significant result for women in South Africa because those women who took part in the workshops intervened and protested the exclusion of women at this important forum. At the first plenary session of CODESA on 13 December 1991, women representing political organizations and parties made historic interventions calling for women's effective participation at the forum. This intervention led to the formation of what is called the Gender Advisory Group.

However, the establishment of the Gender Advisory Group failed to meet the demands of women for effective actual participation. Nevertheless, two major achievements which had an impact on the recognition of gender in CODESA resulted from all these processes. The first is that, given the particular nature of our society, the establishment of the advisory group provided a significant first step towards the recognition of women in the negotiation process. Second, it is of great importance that the Declaration of Intent adopted at this forum characterized the future state as one that is both non-racial and non-sexist. This was a result of women's activities in the country, and was actually a victory for us.

How Women are Organized in South Africa

It is important to describe how women are organized in South Africa, to indicate their strength as an organized force. Like so many other countries, South Africa has always had women's organizations which are structured primarily around their needs in their communities. There are two broad categories of women's movements, and the division is primarily political.

One grouping consists of organizations which, while focusing on gender-related issues, also pursue the broader objective of eradicating apartheid. The other is made up of organizations which focus only on gender-specific issues and proclaim themselves to be non-political. The distinction is important as it affects the power of women as a collective in South Africa to transform our society substantially from one that is inherently racist and sexist to one which is truly democratic and upholds the equality of all people in our society.

Women in South Africa are organized both at the grassroots and at the national level. Common organizational forms at the grassroots level are burial societies and financial societies, the latter also known as *stokvels*. This form of organization is common among millions of black families.

Women have used *stokvel* gatherings for meetings to discuss practical and strategic gender concerns such as power relations between men and women in the family, child care facilities, job opportunities for women, demands for water in squatter areas, and for electricity, and many other issues of a political content. Currently women in these formations are concentrating on the issue of political violence.

There are many other special interest groups of women, such as Rape Crisis and the Coordinated Action for Battered Women (CABW), which are effective at lobbying for their special areas. Religious women's forums are to be found at institutions such as the South African Council of Churches (SACC) and the Institute of Contextual Theology (ICT). These forums were set up during the Decade for Women and they have organized programmes for the promotion of women, following the guidelines of the Strategies for the Advancement of Women (Nairobi 1985). In recent years, women in these forums have played an important role in the anti-apartheid struggle. Since the beginning of political changes, after 2 February 1990, the women's ministries have participated in the campaigns for the protection of protection of women's rights in a new constitution. Other than the SACC and ICT, women's forums in religious bodies deal primarily with charity programmes.

The trade union movement, the Congress of South African Trade Unions (COSATU), has a women's forum, which spearheads gender issues within the programme. COSATU has promoted paid parental leave for workers, fostered the idea of joint parenting, and is currently fighting for the protection of the rights of working children and women in the agricultural and domestic sectors.

There are women's forums or sectors within political organizations and parties. Until recently, the most prominent did not have special forums for women. The ANC and the Pan Africanist Congress (PAC) are the oldest known political organizations with women's forums. Both have pursued a strategy of national liberation with vigour, to the exclusion of addressing gender concerns; however this has changed in the case of the ANC.

The ANC Women's League, formed in 1943, is the oldest women's movement in South Africa. It has undergone transformation with the passage of time. In the 1940s, it focused on the social, political and economic concerns of the disenfranchised. With the banning of the ANC in the 1960s, it subscribed to the broader objectives of the ANC, *vis-à-vis* the overthrow of the apartheid regime. Accordingly, its primary aim was to recruit women for the struggle against apartheid. Qualitative change within the ANC occurred towards the end of the 1980s when women came to regard their struggle as inextricably linked to national liberation. This change came mainly because of the League's participation and increasing exposure over the years in international forums.

Within the organization itself, there was transformation when women moved away from ignoring the struggle for equality of the sexes in deference to national liberation, and actually linked the two. This approach provides the League with the capacity to address gender-specific problems and initiate national programmes relevant to the causes of women. The League has, in fact, set the basis for current developments in the women's movement. At the re-launch of the Women's League on 9 August 1990, after 30 years of exile, it adopted a programme of action which addressed both the political issues and the gender concerns of South African women. One of the most important aspects of this programme is its resolve to network with all women's formations in the country in pursuit of the emancipation of women in a post-apartheid South Africa.

It was on this basis that it launched the campaign for what is today the National Coalition of Women (NCW), which is made up of women from all political parties in the country. On 27 September 1991, the Women's League hosted a meeting of 30 organizations to launch this campaign. The meeting was subsequently followed by regional and local meetings. On 25 April 1992, the organization was formally established at a meeting attended by about 60 national women's organizations and eight regional and local coalitions.

The NCW was formed for the sole purpose of lobbying for a women's charter. For South African women the coalition is a victory, considering that it was formed during very difficult times, i.e., during the struggle for power. But it is, by its nature, a structurally weak organization. Tensions are likely to occur from time to time and cracks will emerge in the Coalition as it mirrors our country. There are many differences of opinion which exist in the broader political milieu that are also found within the National Coalition of Women.

The Campaign for a Women's Charter

Women's organizations in South Africa are energetically discussing women's rights in a future constitution. This is the most prominent activity of women today. When the idea of a charter was first introduced to the alliance, some women's groups rejected the idea for a variety of reasons.

Some women's groups from other parties thought that the ANC was using the League to influence and impose its political agenda on unsuspecting women from these political parties; others were just not familiar with the concept of women's rights. The first step in the process of allaying these fears was to run workshops. These workshops were meant to build trust among women and create a general awareness of women's rights. The approach used was to draw on the experiences of women in other countries as well as to discuss advances made globally in the promotion of women's rights.

We have not fully thought out what the Charter will contain. But we envision a document that will address the demands of women. What is important is that the Charter campaign provides our women with an opportunity of meeting and sharing their experiences. Numerous seminars, workshops and conferences have been held in the past two years at which women's concerns were discussed. They have served the important purpose of uniting women, as illustrated by the CODESA process. It is actually an educational process for the people of our country.

Beyond serving as an effective mobilizing mechanism, there are serious conceptual problems with regard to the content of the Charter. Debates have centred on whether such a Charter will contain all concerns of women as initially perceived, whether it will be part of the constitution, whether this is feasible and, if it is, what would be the implications. One other important aspect of the debate is whether the very notion of an enforceable Charter, embodying exclusively women's rights, does not in fact undermine the position of women by setting them up as different from men.

From the numerous workshops organized to discuss the Charter around the country, concerns raised by women relate to social, economic and political rights. Included among the issues raised by women themselves are domestic violence, rape, sexual harassment, abortion rights, inadequate child care facilities, housing, pension schemes, access to clean water, access to land, access to credit facilities, affirmative action in all structures of a future government as well as the business sector. In other words, the concerns generally take on the historical context of deprivation in our country. I therefore believe that the Charter is likely to embody issues relating to policy formulation as well as to identify concerns which could be characterized as justiciable rights.

The Charter will be an important historic document, invaluable as a political tool for women in my country. Accordingly, it should assume the status of a standard-setting mechanism for promoting equality in our country. If the tradition set at CODESA of consulting women is continued, a Charter could represent a consensus document around which women lobby the constitution-making body to accept it as providing guidelines for the constitution-making process. We envision elections for the constituent assembly or constitution-making body. There is also a possibility that the constitution-making body will consider extra-constitutional agreements or sunset clauses because of the intensity of the power struggle in our country. If this happens, the Charter can be tabled for adoption as one such agreement, in which case it may gain recognition as the basis for formulating social and economic policies while also being retained as an interpretive document for the courts.

The Constitutional Debate in South Africa and Its Impact on Women

In South Africa, the very process of constitution making is an arena in the struggle for power. All energies in my country are focused on determining the best constitutional model for South Africa. There are three main schools of thought in this regard.

First is the separatist approach, pursued by ethnocentrists and neo-fascists, which broadly demands the retention of apartheid. The neo-fascists refuse to enter the arena of negotiations, and advocate the reinstatement of the Verwoerdian model of segregation. The ethnocentrists, on the other hand, would like to see a division of South Africa into national states along ethnic lines which would then merge into a confederation of South African national states.

The second group advocates federalism in South Africa and is made up of centrist and conservative political parties. The centrist section, epitomized by the Democratic Party, urges a move away from a parliamentary system to a system of judicial review. Accordingly, it also proposes a constitution with a liberal form of a Bill of Rights containing only first-generation rights. It is not opposed to constitutional protection of second and third-generation rights, provided these are described as objects of state policy in the constitution. It does not expressly advocate an elected constitution-making body. One can therefore assume that it does not hold any strong opinion on whether CODESA or the constituent assembly should draft the future constitution. It argues for a federal state with maximum devolution of power, a prominent role for business in restructuring the economy, and less government involvement in social and economic structuring.

Within this broad federalist category, the Nationalist Party, the government of the day, is the conservative group. Its proposals are, at best, incoherent. On the face of it, its position is similar in all respects to that of the Democratic Party. However, some National Party proposals at CODESA indicate that it is geared to weaken substantially the central government. The government has embarked on a huge programme of restructuring the country, both socially and economically, thereby forming pockets of power away from the centre. The proposals made by this group are criticized by the left because they are seen as entrenching white privilege; in other words, privatizing apartheid. It is argued that any large attempt at reducing the power of central government would undermine the very concept of equality of all people.

The third category of political opinion is exemplified by the ANC. At the centre of its constitutional proposals is distributive justice as well as a central government with enough powers to enable it to restructure the country. A central tool for change is a Bill of Rights which protects first, second and third-generation rights. This is the most controversial of its proposals.

The most common argument against such a Bill of Rights is that it would be justiciable. The ANC, on the other hand, counters this argument by proposing the establishment of special enforcement mechanisms for the constitution, e.g., an independent constitutional court, a human rights commission and an ombudsman.

At the core of the debate is how best to allay white fears while pursuing a programme aimed at eradicating systemic racial and sex discrimination in our country. The constitutional debate directly affects the Charter campaign as well as the protection of women's rights in a future constitution. Black women in our society are the most oppressed; they suffer race, class and sex discrimination. And since the constitutional process has become a terrain of struggle, they seek substantive protection of their rights in the constitution. The pertinent question, therefore, is how best can the constitution provide *de jure* protection of women's rights.

The answer depends on whether, beyond an equality clause, the Bill of Rights could validly contain women's rights. These can be classified within the category of second-generation rights. Critics of this approach argue that protection of special interest group rights not only diminishes the effectiveness of the Bill, but is an anomaly in a Bill of Rights in the classical sense, because such a Bill protects individual rights against excessive executive power.

If such a Bill of Rights is introduced in South Africa, it will not only serve to protect white privilege, but will also be ineffective in guaranteeing protection of the rights of black people generally and women in particular. Apart from the courts being inaccessible to the majority of the people, the sex and racial prejudice of white male judges is most likely to be reflected in court rulings where a constitutional dispute affecting women or blacks is being judged.

In South Africa, one must look at the entire package of constitutional proposals from the different parties. When you look at all they put together (i.e., a Bill of Rights and decentralized powers) and you add to that what has happened in practice (like the privatization of apartheid by the government's unilateral engagement in the social and economic restructuring of the country), and if you look thus at the fuller picture, you can see that we are actually moving to what one could call 'gender apartheid'. That is a very strong possibility. Therefore, women in South Africa must enter the debate and the struggle over the form of the constitutional debate. When one takes that all together, and looks at the proposed packages, one can see that it is actually a struggle, on one side, to retain privilege and, on the other side, to attain distributive justice. These are the challenges that we face in South Africa.

Political Manipulation of the Future of Women

These, then, are the processes by which women in my country are trying to define what human rights are for themselves. We respect international instruments and in all of our statements we have said a democratic government should actually accede to all international human rights instruments, including the CEDAW (the Convention on the Elimination of All Forms of Discrimination Against Women).

However, there have been recent indications that the present government in South Africa seeks to manipulate international instruments by signing such agreements in order to be accepted and perceived as having changed; in other words, for political purposes. We think these actions undermine our efforts on the ground and we would like to see NGOs protesting against this taking place during the transition period when our people don't even have the most basic right to vote. There are going to be huge protests against this. It also undermines the negotiation process itself because in its preliminary discussions the government has indicated that it does not have to include anything on women. It claims it does not need to use gender-specific words in documents and legal texts, or declare non-discriminatory clauses on the basis of sex. The government says that the CEDAW covers these points and protects women, as do other international instruments. So I think that it undermines our present processes, where we seek first to fix the domestic situation by using the constitutional process to protect women's rights and then have a democratic government (or a properly elected interim government) to accede to international human rights instruments, in order to support these domestic efforts. But now it's being turned the other way around.

Donor Roles and Responsibilities

In regard to the issue of donors, in South Africa an average of 68 per cent of people are illiterate. Of these, two-thirds are women 25 to 35 years of age. Again, one must stress the huge lack of information about women in my country. Little reliable research has been conducted, so there is a lot of work to do. We need to request the international donor community, when they do come into the country, to empower our people to be able to do such research. In my country, there are people who describe themselves as being part of the 'first world' (and I consider that to be really absurd), and describe others in the same country as inhabiting a Third World country. That is a racist statement, but it is the truth – it reflects the divide in my country. So the tendency for donors at the present stage is to look for those 'first worlders' who are already set up at universities and who are the privileged ones. Therefore, I suggest that, if you are developing skills, you should begin with black women and those who are most disempowered, and we will address the needs of the 68 per cent illiterate as well.

I would conclude by appealing to the women of the world: please understand our cause and support us. Those of you who are researchers, can you begin to study and consider some of the questions that I have raised? The most important questions to address are: how can South African women best ensure *de jure* protection of their rights, as well as know what strategies they should employ to bring about actual recognition of their rights? Clearly, we would like to put women's rights in a constitution if that is proper and possible, and we would also like to put social and economic rights in it, too.

From the above it is clear that we have not yet found the best possible way of ensuring substantive protection of women's rights in a post-apartheid era. The world should help South Africans reconstruct a democratic non-racial and non-sexist society that does not perpetuate racism and sexism. Accordingly, donors should affirm blacks and women in their donor programmes in South Africa. Neo-apartheid is a real threat and so is manipulation of the gender question.

5

Special Challenges Confronting Latin American Women

SILVIA PIMENTEL

It is difficult to generalize about such a large and complex region as Latin America. There are certainly common traits, but there are also traits that vary by country, and inside each country because of the huge differences of class, race, and culture. One area of common ground has been the grave economic crisis through which the countries of Latin America have had to pass. Many of our economic problems stem from the aggressive policies of the International Monetary Fund over the external debt.

The socio-economic disparities are great within Latin America. In these countries there is a high concentration of riches in the hands of a few, while the majority of the population live in the worst conditions of poverty and misery. Some of these difficulties are specific to women. The impossibility of paying for private medical services obliges women to depend on the Public Health Service, which is not structured to provide for their needs. So the level of maternal mortality and morbidity is high. What makes the situation worse is the clandestine nature of abortion.[1] The level of sterilizations is high, particularly in certain states in Brazil. For example, 73 per cent of women in the fertile period of their lives are sterilized in the State of Maranhao. According to official data, at least 7.5 million Brazilian women of reproductive age are sterilized – 44 per cent of all women using any form of contraception – and this is a scandal when compared to figures in the First World: the number of sterilizations in Europe is below six per cent of all women using contraceptive methods.

Another common factor among Latin American states is the trend to democratization after years – in some cases, decades – of military rule. The political-social movements created in parties or in independent groups that were searching for democracy provided fertile ground for the political organization of women. Many groups were born of different contexts, with different priorities for action: some have fought to bring down authoritarian power; others are fighting against problems of gender imbalance. This heterogeneity has sometimes created tensions inside the women's movement. If today these tensions have not entirely disappeared, they are at least attenuated and take a different form.

A patriarchal ideology holds sway in the countries of Latin America that are governed by laws based on European codes of the last century, as opposed to the Anglo-American common law system. The juridical system is structured accordingly. As in continental Europe, the normative function is well defined and comes exclusively from the legislative power. The decisions of the judicial power establish rights only for a particular case, even if this decision comes, as is the case in Brazil, from the Superior Federal Court. Formalism and androcentrism are strong characteristics of this system, and are two of the biggest obstacles that the women's movement must confront to achieve their rights.

In criminal law the punitive aspects are emphasized, while the preventive and educative functions of the penal law, which we women stress, are ignored. For example, in the case of domestic violence against women, Brazilian women frequently go back subsequently to the Delegacias de Defesa da Mulher (women's police precincts) to drop the charges because of the relationship they have with their male aggressors, on whom, very often, they depend for survival for themselves and their children. Nevertheless, the 90 Delegacias de Defesa da Mulher spread through Brazil have performed a double service since they were created in 1985, first in providing an avenue for abused women and secondly in opening the question of domestic violence up to debate at the highest level of policy making.

A Triple Emphasis

The emphasis in the Latin American women's movement regarding their rights is upon:

1. Education and consciousness-raising about the need for legal and constitutional change;
2. Studying, debating and drafting normative proposals; for example, during the drafting of the new Brazilian constitution, women coordinated their actions and achieved about 80 per cent of their goals;
3. Education and consciousness-raising about the need to apply existing law, which is often formalistic and abstract, to the concrete situation of women's rights.

Great difficulties appear to complicate women's efforts to establish their rights. Practically all the constitutions of 'civilized nations' lay down the principle that 'all people are equal before the law', and establish their fundamental rights. But the majority of these constitutional norms – as well as the norms contained in the penal and civil codes, for example – have only formal value since some of them are not effectively applied. The law appears as an abstract superstructure, so distant from the daily experience and suffering of women that they are not encouraged to have any dealings with the law. Not only is lawyers' language hermetic and difficult, but the judicial branch of government that should be accessible to the people is not, which makes the law ineffable. Many myths are created regarding this 'law'. One of these myths is, 'What is law is just.' There is an unfortunate contradiction here. The very distance between the people and the law creates an impression of its importance, authority – and justice.

Feminists who work in the legal sphere are sometimes perceived ambiguously by other women. Many grassroots women have difficulty in seeing as important or even valid the work of feminists in law reform. Law is something so distant from the reality of most women's lives that women working to change the laws may not be seen as involved in significant feminist work. Some women who do not believe in the power of the state to provide societal benefits are even more disbelieving about what can be achieved through changes in the law.

The value system in Western civilization still has at its apex the figure of a white, adult, educated and financially secure male. In Latin America especially, the patriarchal family exists in which the *honestidade da mulher* (women's fidelity) is still a precondition of dignity and respect for a woman in society. Conversely, prostitutes are treated as sub-citizens, although prostitution is not a crime in Brazil. One of the issues raised by the small, but growing, number of organizations for the rights of prostitutes is equal rights under the law, or treatment as 'citizens' with respect for their civil rights.

It is not such a simple thing to fight against this paradigm – to deconstruct and reconstruct it according to a utopian feminist philosophy of a more dignified world: a world in which men and women would share their own life experiences based on a new equality between the sexes and respect for difference without hierarchy and without ambiguity. It requires a lot of work and time. Too often young people of both sexes are not interested in critical thinking. Having their attitudes formed mechanically and subliminally in great part by the electronic media, and maintaining conformist attitudes, they feel uncomfortable with the invitation to follow the hard path of deconstruction and reconstruction.

Many legal concepts, inspired by Roman law with its dichotomy between the public and the private, have been questioned by women in recent decades: the notion of head of household, the civil law concept of *patria poder* (patriarchy), family, marriage, women's fidelity, *legitima defensa da honra* (the legitimate defence of honour), rape and others.

A major difficulty that women have in achieving legal change comes from the combination of formalism and androcentrism in our laws. As these laws are structured hierarchically, and as a consistent dogmatic doctrine exists, there is strong resistance to feminist attacks on 'the citadel of the law', which is a source of pride for legal professionals and jurists. The majority of these professionals and jurists are defensive about the law and fail to analyse whether a law is moral or adequate in responding to the claims of society for justice and equity.

Yet in 1988 there came an historic – and beautiful – moment in the women's movement in Brazil when, in the drafting of the new constitution, women's constitutional rights were broadened beyond expectation. Even one of the biggest taboos of Western society, domestic violence, gained explicit mention for the first time in a constitutional text. For in Article 226, which deals with the family, Paragraph 8 establishes the duty of the state to restrain domestic violence and creates mechanisms for doing so. In 1991 Colombia also included such a provision in its new constitution.

However, in the four years of the new constitution, practically nothing has been done to advance this protection at the level of infra-constitutional law. This is not due to any failure of the women's movement to address this area. The women's movement has submitted proposals to change the Civil Code and the Penal Code, and to create other laws to guarantee women's rights. Rather, it is due to the politico-economic difficulties which make the legislature deal with daily crises instead of with necessary structural functions. Many times the legislature has had to halt or contain the excesses of the executive, the President of the Republic. It is also due to a certain incompetence of the legislative branch, and to the rigid structure of the juridical system, which discourages conditions for easy access or rapid action, novelties which would harm the system's patriarchal logic. Nor can one deny that the majority of parliamentarians – and, indeed, the majority of jurists – are not well prepared and keep a distance from the juridical problems of women.

While it is impossible to make mention of all the forces that are being developed in Latin America in support of women's rights, it is worth citing three experiences from my own knowledge.

The Comite Latinoamericano para la Defensa dos Direitos da Mulher (CLADEM) is an organization linking individuals and groups that work for women's rights in the juridical and social spheres. In April 1992 CLADEM sponsored in Sao Paulo a regional seminar on 'Penal Law and Women in Latin America and the Caribbean'. Its conclusions were a good illustration of how women can enrich each other by exchanging information about their programmes and experiences.

The direct result of that meeting has been the development of a draft law specifically on domestic violence, which we are preparing in Sao Paulo based on the experiences of Puerto Rico, Peru, Colombia, and the Province of Rosario in Argentina. This first draft will serve as a point of departure for a broad discussion by the women's movement. Then the draft will be turned into a proposal to be sent to the National Congress, where practically all members of the Women's Caucus have already shown their interest by sponsoring the project.

Secondly, the Centro Feminista de Estudos e Assessoria (CFEMEA, the Women's Centre for Studies and Evaluation), which is based in Brasilia, has commissioned five manuscripts to be published as a series under the title: 'Thinking about our rights: A legislative proposal on non-discrimination'. The areas being addressed are: penal, civil, health, education, and labour. In 1993 when there is a review of the constitution, CFEMEA will be trying to protect the gains made in the 1988 constitution and implement them through the work of the women's movement. It will press for the approval of infra-constitutional norms, a necessary level between the constitutional principles and the social reality.

Thirdly, the Conselho Estadual da Condiçao Feminina do Estado de Sao Paulo (CECF-SP, the State Council of the Status of Women of the State of Sao Paulo) decided to undertake a creative, and probably unique, project. Inspired by the UN Convention on the Elimination of All Forms of Discrimination Against Women, this governmental organ, which was created by women from the women's movement, decided to open for signature a treaty or contract between the mayors of all municipalities and the Governor of the State of Sao Paulo. During the early months of 1992, representatives of the various municipalities in the State of Sao Paulo, together with local leaders and municipal and state administrative organs, searched for and debated definitions of fundamental points of public policy in relation to women, and made themselves responsible for the implementation of such policy. Then, in September, the Governor of Sao Paulo and more than 500 mayors met to sign this document, the *Convenção Paulista Sobre a Eliminação de Todas as Formas de Discriminação contra a Mulher*. In Article 2, this new convention establishes the obligation to make governmental organizations into models for respecting the legal rights and equality of women. The document covers the issues of day care, education, health, labour, and violence. Regarding violence, the document states that 'violence against women is the most tragic manifestation of sex discrimination and it is a duty of everyone who combats or prevents violence in our society to recognize, identify, denounce, and punish physical and social aggression that harms the dignity of the body, of the feelings, and of the image of women.'

Finally, it is important to make clear that, although we are circumscribed by various forces and links among ourselves in Latin America, we consider as fundamental the links between the women's movement on our continent and our sisters in the First World, and also in Africa and Asia. We assume that the social subjugation and oppression of women exist everywhere in the world and we search for ways of overcoming it through solidarity.

NOTE

1 In Brazil, during the drafting of the 1988 Constitution, groups mainly linked with the evangelical and Catholic Churches tried to insert a norm stating that life begins at conception. We feminists managed to find a way to stop this, but we are worried because in 1993 a constitutional revision process begins which could alter some of our feminist provisions, such as this one.

6

Challenges Facing Women in Pakistan

RASHIDA PATEL

When the Constitution of the Islamic Republic of Pakistan was being drafted in 1973 by the National Assembly, the All Pakistan Women's Association sent a delegation to lobby for equality and non-discrimination against women in the new Constitution. I was with this delegation. With the active support of some of the women members of the National Assembly we were able to have inserted in the Constitution the Fundamental Right, namely Article 25(1). All citizens are equal before the law and entitled to equal protection of the law. There shall be no discrimination on the basis of sex alone. But constitutional provisions will not ensure equality for women or political empowerment. This needs constant vigilance and concerted action.

The Constitution places no bar against women voting or standing for any elected position. The veteran leader, Miss Fatima Jinnah, contested the office of President in the 1960s. Recently we had an elected female Prime Minister, Mohatarma Benazir Bhutto. But this did not result in reforms for women, possibly because she was faced with a strong opposition and she did not have stable majority backing.

On the politico-religious platform a controversy has raged as to whether a woman can head an Islamic State. Constitutionally it is a non-issue. Women can contest any of the general seats in the National Assembly; but experience has shown that few women either contest, or get elected to, the general seats. The provision for reserved seats for women lapsed after the 1988 elections. Several women's groups and political organizations have urged a revival of these special seats for women, but the matter is in abeyance as the religious parties are against women in Parliament.

Islamization of the Constitution

For a decade after 1977, Pakistan went through a third period of Martial Law headed by General Zia-ul-Haq, whose stated purpose was Islamization. Various committees and commissions were appointed, and most of their reports recommended that women be barred from the post of head of state. The Ansari Commission recommended that a woman must be at least 50 years of age to stand for election and she must have the written permission of her husband. After women rose in strong protest, these recommendations were discarded.

The Pakistan Women Lawyers Association, with a number of other women's organizations, has filed petitions under the public interest jurisdiction of the Supreme Court challenging several laws which discriminate against women.

In addition, a Federal Shariat Court has been established under the Constitution, and the Court has the power to strike down any law which is repugnant to Islam. In the context of women, the first law to be challenged was that women cannot be judges in an Islamic State. The women's organizations strongly contested this issue and won.

Women's organizations also challenged, as being repugnant to Islam, certain provisions of the *Zinna* (adultery and fornication) Ordinance and the exclusion of female evidence for Hudd punishment. The judgement quoted several authorities against these provisions and also noted the anomalies resulting from the exclusion of female evidence for *Hudd* punishment. However, though clearly giving the finding that *zinna* could not be punished without four eyewitnesses, the Court did not strike down the challenged provisions. An appeal has been filed before the Supreme Court Shariat Bench.

Recently, as a result of judicial activism and the efforts of women lawyers in legal aid and human rights, and of the activities of human rights groups, the Supreme Court of Pakistan has set aside one day a week to hear petitions claiming violations of people's rights. The High Court also takes cognizance of letters as petitions. This is a healthy move for the protection of human rights.

Contrasting Strategies

There are two opposing strategies about Islamization that have been adopted by different groups. There is a strong movement by activists, scholars, and some women's and human rights organizations for a reinterpretation of Islam. They would do this in order to rediscover the intrinsic purity and justice of Islam and to apply it afresh in response to the present needs, and so clearly distinguish it from the historical interpretations that have prevented women from receiving its full benefit.

There is certainly a need for much more research concerning the Islamic rights of women by progressive scholars. The orthodox and obscurantist religious leaders have enjoyed much more time, money and materials, and have had scholars working for them. Progressive scholars are limited in number and have fewer resources.

Another group of human rights and women's associations stand for secular laws and policies. Their contention is that religion is a personal matter and the state has no right to impose religion by law or policy. This movement is limited to a small group of people and, unless there is an economic, social and political revolution, it is unlikely to gain support.

Poverty and Neglect

For the majority of people in the South, the conditions of life are appalling, and women are on the lowest rung. They lack education and training. There is a clear disparity in the levels of literacy of urban and rural women. In Pakistan, an example is the province of Sindh, which is highly urbanized; it has the country's highest literacy rate – 42.2 per cent for urban women – whereas in its rural areas only 5.2 per cent of women are literate.

In higher education, women top the merit lists year after year. Academically they are better than equal, they are superior to men. Yet the percentage of women in universities is much lower than that of male students. This is a natural corollary to the comparatively low percentages of girls in primary and secondary schools.

Training institutions for women are minimal. Most grassroots level training centres for women concentrate on sewing, embroidery, stitching and some arts and crafts – usually without organizing marketing outlets. The institutions ignore agriculture and technology.

In professional colleges the experience in Pakistan is that women are moving to study law, engineering and business. The number of women in the legal profession is increasing impressively. In the province of Sindh one-third of the judicial cadre – that is, civil judges and magistrates at the lower levels – are women, and a few women have reached the levels of session and district judges.

A significantly large number of women from Pakistan are seeking admission to medical colleges. Many female students were being denied admission as they could only compete for the few reserved places. Women activists took the matter up in the courts as a serious case of violation of the fundamental right of non-discrimination on the basis of sex, which is guaranteed by the 1973 Constitution. After a long legal battle the Supreme Court has ruled against the reservation of places in medical colleges and women are now legally entitled to admission on merit.

Women as Workers

In Pakistan the Census Reports and Labour Force Surveys paint a grim profile of women as workers, though the trends are towards an increasing percentage in numbers. These census findings, however, do not reflect the true work of women.

Women do all the housework, which includes cooking, cleaning and caring for the young, the old, the feeble and the ill. It is the woman who brings the water and fuel, often long distances, in addition to undertaking agricultural activities outside the home. In urban areas large numbers of women work in the teaching profession, which is low paid.

In the socio-economic milieu, women are brought up with marriage as their goal. An attitude of dedicated professionalism is often lacking in urban areas. A man's work has priority and the wife often earns much less than her husband. Yet, when the wife works outside the home, she normally fulfils the dual role of housewife and income provider.

Health and Family Planning

Health and family planning facilities are the most neglected area of social services, and this has serious adverse effects on women's health. In Pakistan, with one of the world's highest birthrates, a woman normally bears six to eight children. This leaves little time and energy for herself. An early marriage, a high rate of infant mortality, deaths in childbirth and malnutrition all compound the problem. Information about modern methods of birth control and facilities is available to fewer than 25 per cent of the population and they are mostly in cities. Although contraceptives and sterilization with consent is legal, abortion is a crime in Pakistan, except to save the mother's life. Nevertheless, illegal abortions abound.

The Burden of Attitudes

The attitudes of both men and women multiply the burden of the physical conditions of women's lives. According to family and social tradition, a female is a burden and a liability: her needs have to be provided for; her honour has to be safeguarded. This idea of being a burden is a myth which must be destroyed. A woman's work and her contribution to the home and the family, her productive activities, her invisible labour, her constant striving and sacrifice, her unlimited economic support to her family, community, nation and the world must be systematically projected. People must understand and must acknowledge that they would starve without women's labour. More important, women should realize that they are not mere appendages to men. Women must realize their self-worth.

The practices of dowry and bride-price contribute to the low status of women. Dowry is given to the girl at marriage, so as to assist her husband and family to carry the 'burden' of a wife. A woman is often punished for bringing an insufficient dowry. She may even lose her life, as is reported from India in the many cases of wife-burning.

Legal Status

Women are *sui juris* – independent and responsible for their own actions before the law. Yet there are several conditions, discriminatory laws and practices, inequitable family laws, unhealthy customs and traditions having the force of law, and religious beliefs and edicts that militate against women.

Religion has a strong influence on the people of the South; poverty and ignorance allow religious dogma to be accepted without question. The truth and spirit of religion are often lost. Vested interests find that illiteracy, ignorance, superstition, fatalism and blind faith in the clergy (*Maulanas*) are great allies in the maintenance of the *status quo*. All along, the women's movement in Pakistan has found the obscurantist religious leaders to be its main opponents. In the former Indian subcontinent (now India, Pakistan and Bangladesh), commercial and procedural laws were established according to the British pattern, but the laws governing family and personal life were to be the religious laws of the parties concerned. For Muslims this resulted in the formulation of Anglo-Mohammedan law where misconceived and fossilized Muslim laws based on centuries-old misinterpretations of history became the rule of law. Sadly for the women of Pakistan, the inequities in family law have been difficult to displace, even though there has been consistent pressure for reform.

A major breakthrough was the Muslim Family Laws Ordinance of 1961, which was brought in by the regime of President Ayub Khan, a secularist. It made the registration of *Nikah* (marriage contract) compulsory and provided for a standard form of marriage contract, wherein a woman's rights can be safeguarded and her consent recorded. It restricted polygamy by requiring special permission; it increased the minimum age of marriage for girls to 16 and for boys to 18; and it provided for a procedure involving reconciliation and reconsideration efforts during a period of 90 days before *talaq* (divorce) by the husband becomes final. (However, the latter has been declared un-Islamic and unnecessary in a *zinna* case.)

Although theoretically men and women are to be treated on an equal basis, in practice the law operates against women. The biological aspect, where a woman is pregnant and there is no marriage, operates as evidence against women. There have been some tragic cases where women complained of rape resulting in pregnancy, but they were not believed and were accused and tried under the *Zinna* Ordinance. In cases where the validity of a divorce or remarriage was questioned, it has led to women being put on trial.

The 1984 Ordinance on the Law of Evidence states that there need to be two male witnesses to certify a document; however, if two males are not available, one male and *two* women are required. For a female lawyer this is most embarrassing as, after preparing and advising on the documentation, her signature has only half the value of even an illiterate male. This has not affected the giving of evidence by females in civil cases. However, in trials under the four *Huddod* Ordinances, to award the *Hudd* punishment there must be four adult male witnesses, thus excluding the evidence of females.

Women's organizations and human rights activists have been raising their voices strongly against this discrimination and particularly against the *Zinna* Ordinance, but with little effect. Recommendations to repeal or amend the Ordinance by the Commission on the Status of Women during the Zia regime and by the Women's Legal Rights Committee during the time Mohtaram Benazir Bhutto was prime minister have not been pursued.

Male Support and Opposition

There is some support for the women's movement on several issues from a progressive section of male lawyers, doctors and officials. A news item of 25 August 1992 will illustrate both the support for and the obstructionist opposition of reactionary forces in Pakistan to law reform. Mr Kachkal Ali, a member of the Baluchistan Provincial Assembly, had to tender an unconditional apology on the floor of the house for criticizing the Islamic Laws of Evidence, and for calling the *Huddod* Ordinances and the permission to keep four wives 'suppression of women'. The *maulanas* and *sardars* in the Assembly moved that his speech was contemptuous and tantamount to a desecration of Islamic tenets and a violation of his oath. They declared that his faith was incomplete. They asserted that the Holy Koran allows a Muslim to marry four wives provided he can deal justly with all of them; also that, 'for obvious reasons', the *Shariah* has equated the evidence of two women with that of one man, and *zinna* was punishable when proved by the evidence of four reputable eye-witnesses. Of course, no one went on to note that the law allows a man to marry up to four wives without the means or guarantees to treat them equally or justly, which is never possible. No definition of 'obvious reasons' for equating the evidence of one male with that of two females was given – as if women do not have two eyes, a brain and a tongue like males. And nobody in the Baluchistan Assembly noted that the *Zinna* Ordinance makes *zinna* punishable by Tazir even in the absence of four witnesses. The Pakistan Women Lawyers' Association have written letters pointing these matters out to them.

Liberty, Democracy and the United Nations

Women's issues gained prominence in the South following the independence of some countries in the second half of this century. However, the millions of women who participated in the movements for liberty and democracy found themselves in a society suppressed by discriminatory laws, vested interests, feudal lords and generals. Religion and religious leaders were harnessed to maintain the bonds of poverty and ignorance.

The past 30 years have seen the rise of a movement for women's emancipation. The 1975 United Nations Conference on Women in Mexico City had a tremendous impact on governments and on NGOs, and women's commissions came into being in most countries. However, the women's decade 1975–85 passed, and the shackles on women remained. The situation of women has in fact deteriorated, especially in the developing countries. During the 1980s the most encouraging action from the United Nations was the adoption of the Convention on the Elimination of All Forms of Discrimination Against Women (CEDAW). Unfortunately, a number of countries in the South are not signatories to the CEDAW. The initial momentum in many countries to sign the Convention appears to have abated. There is a need once again to enliven the movement for signing the Convention where it has not been accepted and ratified. In Pakistan, for instance, there has been debate as to whether the provisions of the Convention are in any way repugnant to Islam.

Recently, Pakistan and other Muslim countries signed and ratified the Convention on the Rights of the Child – but with a general reservation that its provisions shall be interpreted in the light of Islamic laws and values. Soon after the adoption of the Convention by the United Nations in 1989, a comprehensive study was conducted at the initiative of UNICEF which showed that no provision of the Convention was in direct conflict with any of the major precepts of Islam, except in the case of adoption, for which a separate provision has been added in the Convention. Although we would like to see the Muslim countries sign and ratify the CEDAW Convention without reservations, a study along the above lines may clear the air for many governments of Islamic countries.

Wars, Trade and Empowerment

Without justice the human rights of women will never be restored. Justice has to happen at all levels: personal, family, community, national and international. At present the exploitative international system, the heavy foreign debt burden, the excessive spending on arms and the military, all leave poor nations with little means for development services and particularly for the attainment of human rights, such as health and education. A new egalitarian economic theory must be evolved to bring prosperity to the poverty-stricken billions. We must press for equality in international trade and international exchanges.

There is a severe neglect of human development. Budgetary allocations show that high percentages of 40 to 50 per cent go for debt servicing and 30 to 40 per cent for defence, leaving little for development. The debt crisis is linked with defence expenditure in that developed countries often give loans for the purchase of arms, or arm one country and thus make it imperative for competing nations to arm. Besides, loans have often not been utilized for development but have been dissipated by bribery and corruption. Often, loans have conditions inserted in favour of the lender. There is some change in recent trends requiring countries that receive loans or aid to spend a certain percentage on the development of women. This concept needs to be underlined.

When countries in the South are torn by ethnic wars and strife, women suffer the worst from disruption. The overt or clandestine supply of arms to different factions obviously leads to increasing tensions and wars. We women must unite for peace.

The question facing us is how do we, as citizens of sovereign nations and as women committed to development, combine our efforts for human rights for women. The CEDAW needs serious attention and much greater projection, for one of the strategies must be organizing to achieve full legal rights for women. Strategies for achieving human rights for women – such as legal awareness, legal aid, vigilance, campaigns for legal reforms – no doubt exist in most countries of the South, but they are on a very limited scale. For instance, in Pakistan with a population of one hundred million people, a small number of such movements cannot have a strong impact. In particular, the campaign for legal reform has to be much more organized, sustained, continuous and far-reaching. It must involve a large section of the people, both men and women. Public lobbying, as seen in the United States, is very limited in our country.

The question remains: how can women affect policies and legislation? There must be political empowerment of women to have a strong voice in the directions which their countries take. The media can play an important role in the political empowerment of women. Radio and television in Pakistan are state-owned, and their policies lean towards orthodoxy with only occasional offerings on themes about women's progress. However, many educated and forward-looking women have been working effectively in the English-language press and have brought up issues of sex discrimination and news of crimes against, as well as success stories of, women. Also, the international media have become more widely available. Since every government wants to show the world that it is progressive and safeguards the human rights of its people and makes pious declarations about how women's human rights are supported, perhaps the scrutiny by the international media of these statements can be harnessed for promoting women's rights.

7

The Challenge of Promoting Women's Rights in African Countries

FLORENCE BUTEGWA

Most efforts to promote women's rights in Africa have concentrated on the domestic front. It is not very helpful to put a lot of effort towards further changes and advances in women's rights if the most basic rights of women are not being recognized and respected at the national level.

African governments commonly use African culture and traditions as an excuse for not amending national laws to recognize women's rights. But a closer look shows that many so-called customs have been discarded – except those that concern women and are meant to subordinate them. There are many examples. A married woman used to have specific rights to her husband's land, but in many communities this is no longer the case. A man can sell property without consulting his wife, disregarding the need to leave sufficient land for food production for the family.

Polygamy is another example of customary practice which has been distorted to weaken the position of the wife. Originally, it was the wife who felt the need for an additional woman to come into the home, perhaps to help with the work or because she was sickly. It was the first wife's prerogative to choose the woman she felt most comfortable with. In fact, one of the essential elements of a subsequent marriage ceremony was the welcoming by the first wife of the co-wife into her home. Nowadays, polygamy is essentially none of the woman's business. A man decides to marry other wives without consulting his wife. The marriage may even be kept secret. In many cases the senior wife and her children are neglected completely or just sent away. Yet many people will argue that this is African culture!

Groups organizing within the African context have approached the issue of women's rights by trying to empower women. Having rights on paper is not going to help women if they cannot exercise them. In addition to rights awareness, there has been an emphasis on mobilizing women, encouraging them to see rights promotion as a community project. Individual women face the danger of social isolation. One common problem is ostracization – a woman who takes her husband to court, for battering her for example, will be shunned by her community, including the women. To counter this potential isolation, women must try to work as a community – if a woman exercises her rights, she should be able to count on the moral and social support of others in the community.

The legal system through which recognized rights are to be enforced presents its own difficulties. Members of the police force often refuse to accept and to record a complaint from a woman against her husband or member of her family. The police treat such complaints as a private family matter. Judicial officers, including judges, have yet to understand women's special concerns and fears. The technical nature of the entire court process – including the pleadings, court language, and the demeanour of the judge and counsel to the process of cross-examination – is a hindrance to the exercise of rights by women. Strategies are needed to make the judicial process a real vehicle for the protection of women's human rights.

In the African context in which we are working, there are few women lawyers. There are even fewer women lawyers with the time and willingness to work with women's rights groups. This is especially so as the work is mostly on a voluntary basis. Many other professional women and grassroots women are actively involved in promoting women's rights. It is disappointing that donors fail to consider this kind of work worth remuneration. They cannot claim to be supporting women's rights work if they refuse to support the many women who make it possible. Male professionals, who are not volunteering, are out there making money while women carry a triple workload – a regular job, unpaid work among grassroots women and their domestic chores.

Women's rights activism now cuts across all disciplines. A knowledge of rights is so essential that we find that groups which focus primarily on income generation are all involved in rights promotion. They cannot make the most of available opportunities unless they know their rights. In Zimbabwe, for example, the leading organization doing legal rights education does not have a single member who is a lawyer but it is doing commendable work. WiLDAF, my own organization, is currently developing a manual for legal rights educators to encourage more women at the grassroots level to get involved. WiLDAF is also training member organizations in using more community-based legal rights educators (paralegals) to empower communities and ensure continuity of the service.

Another strategy is to use international human rights standards in the national fora. The standards set in international treaties and customary law can influence courts at the domestic level. Women's groups are using a country's international obligations as the minimum standard against which national laws should be measured. Gains in this area are slow but significant.

People in developed countries may think that 'organizing' or creating legal rights awareness means simply printing and distributing pamphlets. In Africa this is not always practical as many people, especially women, are illiterate. Radio programmes also have a very limited success rate because the radio is a man's property. In many cases, women do not even have the time to listen to the radio. What is needed is person-to-person contact – being out there, being able to be with the women and talk. But this is not quantifiable and, in terms of most donor criteria, there are few visible outcomes. Sometimes it is difficult to explain that this is slow work, but the resulting social change is an important contribution to the development process.

There is need for research – not for papers to be stored in a library, but research that is action-oriented and will make a difference. For example, women's rights groups have made observations in relation to the selectivity of customs to be retained or discarded, but we have no statistics to back these claims. Grassroots women have the information and they have the ability to document it. What they need is financial assistance.

We have been talking about rights in the juridical sense, but there are other happenings which have a negative impact on women. One example involves the now 'universal' call for environmental protection. The international community is calling for the conservation of forests. But what effect do these programmes have on women? The woman is the person who cooks for the family, and the only source of energy available to her is firewood. Now that forests are sacred she must find another source. There is no electricity or gas. She has neither the technology nor the resources to find alternatives. Some developed countries advise her to plant trees but forget that the land is not hers. Most men would rather grow cash crops. Where does this leave women? They need to grow food and they need to be able to cook it. In the meantime, aid resources are being earmarked for forest conservation without any regard to the development of alternative sources of energy.

We need to look more closely at the programmes being imposed on African countries and to which international loans are applied. Women should be involved in the decision-making process of development strategies and programmes which will affect them, their families and their livelihoods. This is difficult to organize solely at the national level. African women need the support of colleagues in developed countries whose governments are playing a big role in diverting African women's attention from strategic pursuits to the most basic of human wants.

8

Defending Women's Rights –
Facts and Challenges in
Francophone Africa

SÉNY DIAGNE

Women are at the very core of the family unit, whether it is a nuclear or extended family. They are at the centre of all of the family's activities, and have from time immemorial borne the heavy burden of having to feed all of its members.

Consequently, the defence of the rights of women and the emancipation and participation of women in economic, political and social development must be at the heart of any society's inherent concerns.

We know for a fact that more than two-thirds of our agricultural commodities are produced by African women, but they own only five per cent of the continent's wealth, at best. That situation is intolerable and it is society's duty to see to it that women are given their rights and that they can flourish and develop fully. Everyone subscribes unanimously to the idea that, among the criteria used to assess a society's development, the treatment afforded women is the most important.

I will, then, be examining the treatment afforded women in Francophone Africa, past and present, and attempting to see what solutions we can find to improve their status.

The Past

BEFORE COLONIZATION
Officially, the law seemed to view women as objects rather than persons. They were considered to be fragile creatures who were not capable of taking care of themselves and had to be protected from outside dangers.

That view was not universal, however, for in some societies women played a key role. This was the case for certain ethnic groups in West Africa, such as the Akan on the Ivory Coast or the Lebous in Senegal. These societies are matrilineal. In the royal families in Senegal, the Queen Mother had very broad decision-making powers over the affairs of the kingdom.

However, in spite of such exceptions, it must be admitted that the central role played by woman in society was not officially recognized. Women continued to be at the mercy of men's whims and were used to their advantage and to further their ends. Then came the era of French colonization. Was this a plus for African women?

DURING COLONIZATION

The settlers' arrival was a disturbing element, but their influence was limited. Catholic missionaries created a greater turmoil when they preceded the settlers into the remote areas. With evangelization came certain prohibitions – polygamy, for instance, was banned. Overall, however, the settlers' interventions were quite modest. Unless the peace and order of the colonial regime were disturbed, they were content to let things be.

The French civil code did not apply to the vast majority of people. They continued to govern themselves by their own customs, which were listed and catalogued by the French. Thus, women's inferior status was maintained during the colonial period, except for a certain section of the female population who had access to schooling and its benefits.

French women were only enfranchised at the beginning of the century. The women of French West Africa, especially Senegalese women, were also afforded that advantage and were able to vote in the important elections that preceded the independence of various states.

During the 1960s, the decade during which several African states gained independence, there was no progress in African woman's status and well-being. Quite the opposite: African women, during the first two decades following independence, had the distinct impression that their situation worsened. They still had to abide by traditional customs, and these customs often became somewhat mercenary with the monetarization of relations and economic decline. The dowry is a good example: young women became objects of speculation for their parents.

With the advent of International Women's Year in 1975, African governments became more attentive to the fate of women. Laws which improved their condition were passed and ministerial departments for the status of women were created.

The Current Situation

Has the status of women in Francophone Africa undergone any fundamental changes as we near the end of the twentieth century? I feel that it certainly has not. Women in Africa continue to work between ten and 14 hours a day; they continue to suffer from shortages of water and a lack of primary health care. They still have insufficient control over their own reproduction and cannot space out their children; they own a minute percentage of the continent's wealth. What is worse, they have become *de facto* heads of household because men have abdicated their family responsibilities. Drought, structural adjustment and the economic crisis have made the employment situation unstable and farm income uncertain. Men's contribution to household tasks has been declining over the years and has become nonexistent in most households. Thus, women have become responsible for feeding their families and for the education of their children, without really having been prepared for the task.

And yet, legally speaking, a number of things have changed. Legislation furthering the status of women has been passed but these laws seem to have wrought very little change in women's lives, because of illiteracy and a lack of information.

Family Law

FORCED MARRIAGES AND CONSENT

Current African laws all hold that consent is a prerequisite if a marriage is to be considered valid. Do African social mores reflect that fact? Unfortunately, the answer must be no. This is due to the resistance of traditional practices to written law. Traditional authorities feel that women should not have anything to say in the matter and should be ready to accept the husband their parents have chosen for them, since it is believed that parents could not make the wrong choice. That belief is deeply embedded in the traditional African psyche.

PREMATURE MARRIAGE

In spite of legislation stipulating that girls shall be considered nubile between 15 and 18, young girls (children, in fact) continue to be married at the ages of nine, ten, eleven or twelve, while they are still busy with childhood, games, grade school. In this way, both their childhood and their future are confiscated. They have very early pregnancies and there is a high mortality rate among this group, as they die from complications following pregnancy or in labour. It is imperative that we take action quickly against these premature marriages.

POLYGAMY AND DOWRIES

These two institutions have historically been a feature of African society. Dowries are an institution that is deeply anchored in the African consciousness and attempts to eliminate them would run into insurmountable obstacles. The few African laws that have attempted to limit dowry amounts through specific regulations are steps in the right direction. The next phase should be to make everyone in our society aware of the existence of these laws and of the sanctions that can be applied if they are violated.

As for polygamy, the equation is even more complex. There is no doubt whatsoever that it contributes to the violation of women's rights; but it is more or less accepted by African women. It is accepted by rural women because the arrival of a second wife means a certain lightening of their domestic burdens. City women are also coming to a greater acceptance of polygamy because for them it means liberation from the servitude of marriage; a wife can go about her own business when she is not on duty, without having to worry about the care and feeding of her husband.

That being said, should polygamy then be eliminated? I think that there should be an awareness-raising campaign to bring about change in customs and attitudes, while maintaining the progressive gains that have been made in certain countries, for instance in Senegal, where people have a right to choose between monogamy and polygamy.

HEADING THE FAMILY AND EDUCATING CHILDREN

Nearly everywhere in Africa, men are not only the nominal heads of households but they are the sole holders of parental power. These provisions clash head-on with reality. Because of hard economic times and a certain evolution, women are more and more inheriting the mantle and the prerogatives of heads of households. It would only be fair to incorporate that fact into legislation by providing for joint family leadership and replacing paternal power with shared parental power.

DIVORCE

In many jurisdictions in Africa, laws have made divorce legal in order to counteract a practice that has been denounced by all women: repudiation. Appearing before a judge should allow women to defend their interests and those of their children better. The reality encountered by women does not match up with these expectations, but there is no doubt that legalizing divorce is a step in the right direction, that of better protection for women's rights.

As for the custody of children after a divorce, the current practice in all African patriarchal societies is to assign the responsibility to the father or his family. Child custody should instead be determined by a single overriding concern: the best interests of the child. Here again, the judge's intervention will act as a counterweight to the traditional customs and practices that tend to deprive women of their children.

CUSTOMS AND WOMEN'S ESTATE RIGHTS

African traditional laws generally prevent women from inheriting anything at all from their husbands, which causes some very acute and dramatic problems. Worse than that, though, is the fact that women themselves are often considered as chattels of the estate, as though they were cows, houses, or chairs. The law forbids that sort of behaviour and, if conflicts are settled in court, the judge's decision will be made according to law. But customs are powerful and enduring, and often, if not always, women are unaware of their rights and of the possibilities the law offers them.

Women and human rights organizations must mobilize to fight tooth and nail for the complete abolition of these customs and for the enactment of legislation that confirms that women and men have the same rights where inheritances are concerned. The dignity of women is at stake here.

The Right to Health

Health, according to the World Health Organization, is not only the absence of disability or illness but can be defined as 'a state of physical, mental and social well-being'. Can a woman who works 12 to 14 hours a day, who gives birth to a child every year and who has no way of obtaining even the most rudimentary health care, attain a state of physical, mental and social well-being? The answer is a resounding no.

It is true that the vast majority of Africans do not have access to health care, but women are by far the most underprivileged group. They fall victim to endemic diseases, they rarely can find the time to go to the few health centres that do exist, and they also fall victim to rape and violence.

WOMEN'S ENDEMIC DISEASES

The main endemic diseases that African women suffer from are malaria, sexually transmitted diseases, breast cancer and cancer of the uterus, and vaginal fistulas. Women spend many hours each day farming in the fields or looking for fuel wood in the bush, thus becoming prime targets for malaria-transmitting mosquitoes. These are the most serious diseases but they are not the only ones: cholera, dysentery, diarrhoea are also causing extensive damage, as well as the plague of this century, AIDS.

STERILITY, FAMILY PLANNING AND SEX EDUCATION

For the African woman, being sterile is like being a leper. The African woman who does not have children is treated in an inhuman and degrading way. Women are considered child-bearers before being considered women. Organizations that defend the rights of women must also take up the defence of sterile women, but those women also need information: many types of sterility can be cured and family planning may help.

Something can be done to stop this scourge. Particular emphasis must be placed on sexual education; we have to struggle to demystify sex and overcome traditional religious taboos in order to provide early sex education to girls and young women, educated or not.

RAPE AND VIOLENCE

In countries like Senegal, legislators have introduced more severe penalties for rapists, especially those who rape minors of less than 13 years of age. This legislation should be combined with an education campaign aimed at those who intervene after a rape has been committed, i.e., police, physicians, judges. Since rape is an offence which is very difficult to prove, it is only with the help of all of the above-mentioned parties that women will be able to prepare airtight cases against rapists which will lead to their conviction. As for domestic violence, a specific offence must be created with a shorter procedure that will allow the battered wife or girlfriend to act quickly.

It is worth mentioning, however, that the African community, and perhaps the global community, do not realize how widespread these two scourges are and that is why an awareness-raising campaign on a large scale is needed.

The Right to Work

THE SALARIED FEMALE WORKER

All African laws guarantee equal pay and equal working conditions to women. In this way, they are a reflection of state constitutions, which proclaim that there shall be equal pay for equal work. One can only applaud the fact that the legislation exists, but the reality which women encounter is not as favourable.

Furthermore, women who receive salaries pay the same contributions to social programmes as men and yet they do not receive family allowances; nor, in the event of their death, do their heirs receive survivor benefits. Indeed, should the female worker die, her heirs will receive nothing from the sums that were withdrawn from her salary for pension purposes.

Again, it is urgent that we fight against the insidious job discrimination that exists in workplaces: whenever any type of promotion is offered, men are always chosen over women for specious reasons. Women must increasingly protest against such decisions. Perhaps we should consider quotas, and adapt that solution to each country.

WOMEN IN THE INFORMAL SECTOR

Seventy-five to 80 per cent of women work in the informal sector in Francophone Africa. That sector is by definition unstructured, but we must protect the women who work in it, nevertheless. If those women are to be protected, we must help them organize so that they are able to take responsibility for themselves. They have institutions such as the *tontines* that can serve as informal banks if appropriate regulations govern their operations. What has been done in Benin in that regard should be undertaken in all Francophone countries.

As for medical and social protection, credit unions should be created in all parts of the informal sector for the purpose of meeting the needs of female contributors.

SEXUAL HARASSMENT

The phenomenon is not new in the workplace but it has certainly been exacerbated by the economic crisis. As work has become rarer, some men have taken advantage of the situation to impose degrading conditions on women.

How can we fight against sexual harassment? As a first step, a new offence needs to be created in order to curtail it, as the range of offences that exist in our various criminal codes will not allow us to do that effectively. Secondly, we need to make women themselves (and the rest of society) more aware of this situation.

Political Rights

REALITIES OF POLITICAL LIFE

Women make up at least 51 per cent of the population in all countries in Francophone Africa, which means that they form the majority of the electorate as well. But what does one see? A mass of women who sing, dance and liven up the political meetings; and when all is said and done, only a handful of women have been elected. And, when they do get elected, they are given the least important positions.

THREE OBSTACLES TO POLITICAL SUCCESS

Women's lack of self-confidence is undeniably the most important of these obstacles. Since they have always played supporting roles, they remain convinced that they cannot play leading roles in politics. Women's organizations have a role to play here in that they must help women to overcome their self-doubt by showing them that they can indeed assume any of the roles that men currently hold. Another obstacle is a lack of solidarity among women. Manipulated by men, they are involved in constant infighting, to the detriment of their cause. The last obstacle is women's lack of political knowledge and experience. Better training and information is needed to upgrade women's political literacy.

The Challenge: Strategies to Protect Women's Rights Effectively

It goes without saying that, as we near the end of the twentieth century, women cannot continue to be illiterate and unaware of their rights.

A MASSIVE LITERACY PROGRAMME

More than 80 per cent of African women are illiterate, and yet we live in a technological and scientific world. Women must be able to benefit from technological and scientific progress. They can only do so if they know how to read and write. Consequently, public authorities should launch massive literacy campaigns, putting particular emphasis on women. For women, becoming literate is really the key that will give them access to the modern world and to progress. Donor agencies have a very important role to play in that agenda; they would get a good return on their investment in literacy programmes, because any investment made in women in Africa can only be profitable.

ESTABLISHING LEGAL INFORMATION AND DOCUMENTATION CENTRES

Legal information centres have become commonplace in Anglophone African countries but they are still fairly rare in Francophone Africa. The importance of those centres is now an accepted fact; since women must take the lead in defending their rights, they must first of all know those rights. Since legal texts tend to be hermetic, women need to be able to understand them. The laws must be explained to them in everyday language and that is the role of legal information centres.

ENCOURAGING FEMALE CANDIDATES TO RUN

All women in French Africa have the right to vote and the right to run in elections. They are very active in political parties, especially in the multi-party context. Women have to become organized and form committees to support female candidates. These groups should not only encourage female candidates to run but also provide moral and financial support once they declare their candidacy. The committees would also be responsible for awareness-raising and for training other women to elicit a gender consciousness and solidarity that would lead them to vote massively for their sisters.

LOBBY GROUPS FOR LAW REFORM

Both national and regional solidarity will be needed to support either law reform or the enforcement of existing laws granting certain rights to women. Women do not enjoy those rights in reality, because of the pressure of religious or social customs and traditions.

At the national level, all women's organizations and women's rights advocacy groups must come together to create an umbrella organization which would be responsible for coordinating the various aspects of the struggle to defend women's rights. To be more effective, however, that umbrella organization should not carry on the struggle by itself; good links should be built among all of the lobby groups in Africa (whether Francophone or Anglophone) and with all other countries of the world.

Regionally, a network advocating and defending women's rights throughout Africa must be built to help us seize the future. It would be unrealistic to think that women in every country can defend themselves in isolation. Because of the speed of communications and of the various regional and sub-regional integration projects afoot, it is obvious that building strong and reciprocal links in anticipation of the economic or political union of these various countries will serve the interests of women. Once coordination has been achieved at the regional level, a network must also be created among all of the international women's rights advocacy organizations.

TYING INTERNATIONAL AID TO WOMEN'S RIGHTS

All international organizations and Western countries who provide funds to Africa should make greater respect for women's rights a condition of any international aid. Efforts to foster democracy through aid conditionality have succeeded beyond all expectations. Similar efforts of the same degree should be extended to women's rights, all the more so since almost all African countries have ratified the international conventions against sexual discrimination.

Asking countries to implement the conventions which they have ratified would only be fair and would not in any way constitute interference in the internal affairs of these countries. Women are an important driving force in any development in Africa; they produce 75 per cent of the agricultural food products. If women are encouraged to develop and flourish, the nation as a whole is helped. Of course, we live in a man's world where men do not want to lose their privileges, but it has been demonstrated clearly that development efforts that exclude women are doomed to failure.

Countries and organizations that provide funds should therefore demand that any project submitted to them for financing pay particular attention to women. Each project should take the specific interests of women in our communities into account in order that those women may derive maximum benefit. Some countries, like Canada and the United States, have begun to apply that policy, albeit somewhat timidly. The policy must be applied in a more aggressive and forceful way, so that those who draft and submit any project know that, should their project not take women into account, no funding will be forthcoming.

9

Women Living Under
Muslim Laws

MARIE AIMÉE HÉLIE-LUCAS

The North–South axis implies that on the one hand there is 'development' – culture, wealth, democracy – and, on the other (ours), there is poverty, stagnation, helplessness and dictatorship. The one-way road from us to the other is that of 'progress'; and from the other to us is 'aid'.

Two monolithic blocs facing each other. . . .

My understanding of the world is that there is not one axis, but many. Initiatives come from all sides and we have to look for potential allies outside, while struggling from within.

The Women Living Under Muslim Laws network does not have a 'North–South' conception of the world. Set up by women from Muslim countries and communities, it believes that strengthening women, here or there, South or North, will ultimately strengthen us all.

The extreme right movement in the US or in Europe, with its strong stand against women's rights, is by no means alien to its equivalent in Muslim countries. All types of fundamentalism target women in the name of identity and moral order.

Unless we all see these connections, as well as the connections between what women gain in whatever part of the world, we may not step out of the North–South axis or break the false dichotomy. We will go on speaking the language of 'aid', although it is high time we spoke the language of solidarity.

Women who live in Muslim countries and communities are, like women everywhere, actively engaged in promoting positive change – oppressed, no doubt, but not helpless.

The Context: The Myth of a Homogeneous Muslim World

About 500 million women presently live in Muslim countries and communities, the majority in Asia (Indonesia is the largest Muslim country in the world). Islam is also rapidly expanding throughout Africa, while the Arab countries, where Islam originated, now only represent a minority of the Muslims in the world. Because Islam operates in so many economic, political and cultural situations, the circumstances of women living in all these varied contexts will obviously present differences. The various schools of thought in Islam look at the subordination of women in different terms. Also, Islam, while expanding, has absorbed local traditions. This variety in interpretations of religion, as well as in indigenous culture and traditions, obviously has repercussions on women's lives and rights; but, above all, there is a political use of both religion and culture.

Female genital mutilation, for example, is a tradition in a specific African region, close to the ancient Egyptian area. The practice is unknown to Muslims in other parts of Africa or in Asia. It is practised on all women, be they Christians, Animists or Muslims. However, under the pressure of local *mullahs*, Muslim women from this region are made to believe that this practice is part and parcel of being a Muslim, and therefore unchallengeable.

Veiling is a semitic tradition in the Middle East which is not practised in other Muslim areas in Africa and Asia. The caste system, inherited from the Hindu tradition, is applied only within the Muslim community in India.

These few examples give a fair idea of the diversity in the Muslim world. Interaction between women from different Muslim societies has shown that 'while similarities exist, the notion of a uniform Muslim world is a misconception imposed on women'.[1]

In fact, our different realities range from being isolated and voiceless within four walls, subjected to public flogging and condemned to death for presumed adultery, and forcibly given in marriage as a child, to situations where we have a far greater degree of freedom of movement and interaction, the right to work, to participate in public affairs, and to exert a greater control over our own lives.[2]

It is thus of prime conceptual importance to speak not of Muslim law (singular), but to express the plurality and diversity of these situations by referring to Muslim laws (plural).

Because women are isolated in their own national context, they have no means of challenging the validity of what is imposed on them in the name of religion. Exchange of information from one Muslim country to another is therefore a key element for women in legitimizing their struggles for women's human rights.

For instance, the fact that Muslim countries have such different policies regarding reproductive rights is in itself enlightening for women. Algeria refused for 20 years even to allow knowledge about contraception and abortion; the Algerian government finally changed course on contraception when the population's growth rate reached 3.5 per cent, threatening ruling class privileges. Tunisia offers both contraception and free abortion services to women; and in Bangladesh there is forced contraception, abortion and sterilization. In all these countries, political leaders pretend to act in conformity with Islam, while they are simply imposing a political solution on their population problems.

Equally interesting is the fact that traditions which are favourable to women are eradicated and replaced by practices inherited from colonization. For instance, women in the Arab world used to be called by the name of their father throughout their lives (e.g., Fatima bent Mohamad or Fatima daughter of Mohamad). Recently, legal measures have been introduced which force women to bear the name of their husbands. This means that in countries with high rates of divorce and repudiation where women may undergo several marriages in a lifetime, a woman may have to change her name several times, resulting in a loss of identity. This shows that although self-proclaimed 'Islamic' states pretend to regain their identity by rejecting all Western elements imposed on them through colonialism and imperialism (especially when it comes to women), they do not mind incorporating Western traditions which deprive women of an element favourable to them in the Arabo-Muslim culture.

Unless women can communicate within the Muslim world, they cannot compare the changes occurring in their own country with those in other countries, and therefore are not even able to dream of a different reality. As the Aramon Plan of Action states, 'Depriving us of even dreaming of a different reality is one of the most debilitating forms of oppression we suffer.'

Neither can Muslim women differentiate in their oppression between what pertains to culture, to religion or to politics, and therefore they cannot challenge these changes.

Within the diversity of the economic, cultural and political contexts, it is striking to see that similarities tend to be confined to the private sphere, to the domain of the family, and that women in so many places are deprived of human rights and civil rights, more especially so within the frame of Muslim Personal Laws (also called Family Codes).

The Legal Situation of Women in Muslim Contexts

The legal situation of women living in Muslim countries and communities has been deteriorating over the past two decades through the process of Islamization, i.e., the creation of 'Islamic' states. A certain version of Islam (best known in the media as 'fundamentalism') is being promoted and is expanding, mainly to the detriment of women.

Failing to set up anything specifically Islamic in their politics or economics, 'Islamic' states turn to their only specificity – making women the guardians of culture and religion and confining them to a model and a way of life which is 14 centuries old.

Their focus on Family Codes is crucial to the deterioration of women's lives. Family Codes set the rules for aspects of life which affect women: marriage, polygamy, divorce, repudiation, custody and guardianship of children, sexual control, reproductive rights, inheritance, and testimony in court.

In 1984 in Algeria, for example, women lost the right to marry. They now have to be given in marriage by a *wali* (matrimonial tutor) and are considered minors throughout their lives. Polygamy and oral repudiation have become legal for men, whereas women cannot initiate divorce (except in very few codified instances). Women cannot be the legal guardians of their children; they may have temporary custody of the young ones only, under the control of their ex-husbands and under very restrictive conditions. In addition, women have an unequal share in inheritance.

In 1984 in Egypt, women lost the right to stay in the matrimonial home after divorce or repudiation – it was a right they had won previously after a decade-long struggle.

In 1986 in India, women from the Muslim community lost the right to maintenance after divorce. This bill – ironically called 'Muslim women's protection of the right of divorce bill' – applied only to Muslim women and was passed by a supposedly secular state bowing to pressure from Muslim men. It unconstitutionally discriminated against a specific section of the Indian female population.

In 1989 men in Algeria were delegated the right to vote on behalf of their women relatives.

In Pakistan, women are still struggling against the *Huddod* Ordinances which condemn 'adulteresses' to death by stoning or 100 lashes. Recent research conducted by women lawyers and social scientists shows that thousands of women wait endlessly in jail for their trials, accused of *zinna* (sex outside marriage). This allows husbands and other family members to get rid of them while they settle – to their benefit – questions of remarriage, property or inheritance.

On 15 April 1990, Iraq passed a decree allowing men to kill their womenfolk for adultery. No mention was made of any need to prove adultery; men received from the state the extraordinary privilege of being both judge and executioner of women in their families, without recourse to justice for the accused.

And we should not forget that Shariah law was recently passed in the Sudan, Pakistan and Bangladesh – a version of Islam selected by rightist men – that curtails the rights of women. These laws institutionalize supposedly Qur'anic practices by making them the law of the state; the state thus intervenes actively on behalf of men, in the private lives of women.

Even more important than these isolated instances illustrating the erosion of women's human rights is the fact that, within the Arab world and South Asia, there are organized attempts at uniformization of 'Family Codes'. Three sessions of the South East Asia Shariah Conference have been held to unify all Muslim Personal laws in South East Asia, while the justice ministers of Arab countries have been meeting regularly over the past decade for the same purpose.

What fundamentalists are openly advocating is 'separate development' for women, a policy that was opposed the world over when applied to blacks in South Africa under the name of 'apartheid'.

Women are becoming increasingly aware of the expansion of a 'hard' version of Islam, generously financed from different sources, which tends to promote laws unfavourable to women and eradicate those to their benefit. Tunisian women now benefit from a quite egalitarian Family Code – a favourable situation – which they may lose if uniformization takes place in the Arab countries. Women in Muslim countries and communities are trying to thwart the 'worst scenario' now increasingly being imposed by rightist forces throughout the Muslim world, while promoting at the same time the 'best scenario'.

The 'Women Living Under Muslim Laws' Network

In this context, women felt the need for an international network to link women from different Muslim countries and communities across continents. Initial impetus came from urgent cases in 1984 requesting solidarity action: in Algeria three feminists were jailed and kept incommunicado for seven months for having educated other women on the proposed Algerian Family Code which was intended to reduce women's rights severely. In India, a woman filed a petition to the Supreme Court challenging the constitutionality of her divorce by oral repudiation, allowed by the Muslim Personal Law. In Abu Dhabi, a pregnant domestic worker from Sri Lanka (who subsequently gave birth and cared for the baby in jail) was sentenced to death by stoning. In Europe, the Mothers of Algiers (women divorced from Algerian men and seeking access to or custody of their children, denied to them for many years) marched from Paris to Geneva to present their case to the Commission of Human Rights of the UN.

The WLUML network was therefore created in 1986, and is based within Muslim countries and communities in Asia, Africa and the Arab world. However, it has been increasingly confronted with the problems of women of Muslim descent living in Europe and the Americas, and of women who are not Muslims but are affected by Muslim laws through citizenship or their marriage and children.

The WLUML network undertakes to:[3]

- Exchange information within the Muslim world on women's specific situations (their similarities and differences), their struggles and their strategies. This allows women to become aware of the general political trends threatening them; break their ideological isolation; confront on their own terrain the various political, cultural and religious elements which contribute to their oppression; learn about their legal and religious rights and about differences within Islam, possible interpretations of it and currents within it; and prioritize issues.

- Actively support women's initiatives in Muslim countries and communities and defend women's human rights. All requests from groups and individuals seeking support and urgent action for reform or defence of women's rights are forwarded throughout the network. These include campaigns for the repeal of discriminatory legislation, an end to oppressive practices, the enactment and/or enforcement of legislation favourable to women or cases of systematic and generalized violations of women's human rights as well as individual cases where, for example, inhumane sentences have been given to women, women have been forcibly married, fathers have abducted their children, or women have had their lives threatened. It is to be noted that since jurisprudence is essential in Islam, cases won on behalf of women are of utmost importance and serve as landmark cases.

- Organize collective projects. Women participating in the network define priority actions, share the tasks and implement projects aimed at changing women from passive recipients of information to active producers of useful knowledge. Collective projects involve women throughout the network, they build on one another and feed into each other.

At the formal founding of the WLUML network at the Aramon meeting in 1986, women felt a need 'to share living and contextual experiences'. Towards this end, we organized the first exchange programme for women in the Muslim world in 1988. The intention was to allow women activists an opportunity to travel and interact with their counterparts in other Muslim countries and to see the broad spectrum of possible strategies used in different parts of the Muslim world.

Identifying what pertains to customs, and what to religion, and the political use of both, helps us 'separate the threads which have been woven together to form a particular garment which women have to wear willingly or unwillingly', as stated in Background and History of WLUML.

Drawing from this first encounter and shared experiences, women in the WLUML network thus decided to initiate the two following common projects:

- to identify and challenge different interpretations of religious texts and to promote women's interpretations;

- to compile and compare laws drawn from these interpretations, which primarily affect women.

The Qur'anic Interpretation by Women working meeting in July 1990 in Karachi, Pakistan, allowed women to see just how differently the same verses of the Qur'an have been interpreted both through translations and explanations (*tafsir*) by Islamic scholars and schools of thought. The discussions revealed that, throughout history, individuals and groups have continued to use the principles of *ijtehad* and *ijmaa* to interpret the tenets of Islam in the light of changing circumstances, new knowledge and needs.

Through a collective reading of the verses, participants realized that there are alternative interpretations for the verses that have been used to limit women's rights to self-assertion and control over their own lives and environment, especially when translated into state or community laws. An ongoing research group has been set up and continues to work together in order to serve the needs and answer the questions confronting activists. There is a strong need to create space for reflection for those women who can only operate within a religious framework and cannot support women's human rights from a secular point of view; these women must be offered alternatives to becoming the easy prey of the growing religious right.

While the Qur'anic Interpretation meeting allowed women an alternative interpretation, the Women and Law Program (started in 1991 and continuing until 1994) explores and analyses the laws and their application in the broader socio-political and cultural domains. As we know, laws are derived from customary, religious, social and political sources, each contributing its share towards denying women their legitimate rights. We are aware that there are those who desire to expunge customs from the laws and elaborate an exclusive code to be imposed on all. This is not our objective. We are not bound by either customs or interpretation. In both there is diversity within which we are searching for space to reformulate laws based on social justice.

Our research involves women (activists, lawyers and theologians) in 24 Muslim countries and communities in Asia, Africa and the Middle East, and will culminate in the production of an international handbook for grassroots activists. On the one hand, this will translate legal terminology into everyday language; on the other hand, it will provide all possible practical information in comparing the various forms of Muslim Laws, groups/ individuals who have challenged their inhumane aspects, the strategies used and their success. We also hope to collectively identify legal points through which women could put pressure on authorities.

'By pooling our knowledge and resources together we can avoid the worst scenario and at the same time promote a more just environment. We fear that if we do not act, we may be subjected to a situation which will not necessarily be the worst but could certainly be worse than what we have today . . .'[4]

In a worst scenario:[5]

- unilateral and oral pronouncement of *talaq* (repudiation) would be legal, as currently exists in India;

- women's right to vote would be delegated to men, as in Algeria;

- *zinna* (adultery and fornication, i.e., extramarital sex) would be punishable by stoning to death or public flogging, and/or a fine, and/or imprisonment, as in Pakistan;

- women orally repudiated by their husbands, and therefore having no proof of their divorce, could be sentenced under *zina* if they re-marry;

- *zinna bel jabr* (rape) would require 'the eye witness account of four male adult Muslim men of good repute' before the rapist could be given maximum punishment, as is currently the case in Pakistan;

- women would be tried and executed for un-Islamic behaviour – for instance, laughing in the streets and/or allowing a strand of hair to fall out of the *hidjab* – as has already happened in Iran;

- women would be subjected to forcible contraception, abortion and sterilization, as in Bangladesh;

- women would not have the right to drive, as in Iran and Saudi Arabia;

- women would not have the right to vote, as in Kuwait;

- women would be circumcised as in Egypt, Somalia, Sudan;

- women would be forcibly given in marriage by their male guardians (*wali*), as in communities governed by the Maleki and Shafi schools.

None of these laws exist in all Muslim countries, nor are they intrinsic to Islam. On the other hand, we would like all women to enjoy the following rights which exist in at least some Muslim countries:

- the right to vote at all levels, as in most Muslim countries and communities;

- the right to choose their own husbands, as in countries governed by the Hanafi school;

- the right to divorce, as in Tunisia, or at least the delegated right of divorce (*talaq-e-tafweez*) as in Pakistan and Bangladesh;

- the right to a share of the marital property upon divorce, as in Malaysia;

- the right to custody and guardianship of their children after divorce, as in Tunisia;

- the right to the marital home at least until the children are adults, as in Libya;

- the ban on polygamy, as in Tunisia;

- the right for a wife to curtail second marriages, as in Bangladesh, Pakistan and Singapore.

The Women and Law Program, as stated in the Program's Guidelines for

Coordinators, 'also aims to empower women living under Muslim laws through knowledge of their rights in their societies and to strengthen their capacity to understand their situations, to act locally, and work together towards meeting their needs. As well, it aims to enhance the participation of Muslim women in the development of their societies.'

The following two examples demonstrate how these objectives can be achieved. In 1987, in Sri Lanka, a case drew public attention to issues related to maintenance and alimony for divorced women. As a result of this particular case, the government set up a committee to look into this aspect of Personal Laws reform. The Sri Lankan Muslim Women Research and Action Front (MWRAF) requested the WLUML network to send material and information on progressive laws in other Muslim countries and communities. Based on this information, MWRAF was able to present a memorandum[6] and campaign for local support. Two women for MWRAF were subsequently invited to participate in the drafting of the proposal for reforms to the Muslim Marriage and Divorce Act. They have been members of the Commission ever since.

In 1989, a similar situation arose in Mauritius when the main opposition party, the Muslim party, was pressuring the government to amend the constitution to allow the reintroduction of Muslim Personal Law; this would have discriminated against women from the Muslim community by depriving them of the rights they would have enjoyed as citizens of Mauritius under the common civil code. The rest of the female population would not have been affected.

Making use of the abundant documentation sent by the WLUML network in response to the urgent request of the Mauritian group Muvman Liberasyon Fam, the reintroduction of Muslim Personal Law has been rejected; at present the civil code still prevails, providing equal rights to all women in Mauritius.[7]

Circulation of information, supporting each other's struggles, drawing on each other's strategies, and collective projects are the basic activities of the WLUML network.

Constraints in Implementing Projects of the 'Women Living Under Muslim Laws' Network

We should first say that although some of the constraints we are facing may be specific to the environment in which the WLUML network operates, we believe that they are similar in many ways to those faced by women's organizations elsewhere.

The outside world tends to identify women from Muslim countries and communities with oppression and helplessness – a lost cause. Dispelling this image is one of the challenges we face. Indeed, there is increasing oppression, but women living in Muslim countries and communities are active on all possible fronts. All women face difficulties in having their rights recognized as human rights, but it seems even more difficult for women in Muslim contexts because authorities in many countries use various pretexts to refuse help. For example, in 1988 a 20-year-old Algerian woman, born and raised in France, took refuge in a women's shelter after filing a case against her father and elder brother who severely beat her, isolated her, and wanted to marry her off to an unknown man in Algeria. However, she was kidnapped from the shelter and illegally driven to Algeria through Spain and Morocco. She was drugged and beaten, her identity papers were taken from her, and a marriage contract was signed, with the ceremony planned for the following month. Fortunately, she was rescued in time, thanks to women networkers who found her, took the case to court in Algeria and won.

It should be noted that French authorities refused to handle the case. A written statement from a government minister (a woman) to the WLUML explained that 'France could not interfere in Algerian private affairs'. Interestingly enough, dealing with a criminal offence, that is, a kidnapping on French territory, was in this instance considered interference in the affairs of a sovereign neighbouring country. No other crime committed on or by males – Algerian, French or other – on French soil would ever have been seen that way.

Similarly, when a decree was passed in Iraq allowing men to kill alleged adulteresses within their families, a respectable international human rights institution felt that the case fell outside its mandate. Yet such an official delegation of power from the Iraqi Ministry of Justice to allow males to be both judge and executioner clearly indicated government responsibility for the killing of alleged adulteresses – a situation which indeed fell within that organization's mandate.

This trend to 'respect' other cultures and/or religions is generally to the exclusive detriment of women: when the *Hudd* punishment is pronounced and a thief's hands are cut off, there is an outcry from the international community, but when the genitals of a girl are cut off, the fear of interfering in another culture prevails. When apartheid condemns blacks in South Africa to racial segregation, there is an outcry from the international community, but when extreme right movements condemn women 'in the name of Islam' to 'separate development', the international community remains silent.

All the examples cited prove that it is hardly a question of religion or culture but rather of politics. In this context, linking aid to the democratization of our countries gives us little hope, since there is no sign that the fate of women will be seen as a valid indicator of democracy by the international community. What we see instead is a narrow interpretation of democracy in the exclusive sense of parliamentary democracy. This never prevented Hitler from being elected!

Rather than leaving women to the 'goodwill' of their (male) political leaders, states should be obliged by donors to direct a percentage of their aid money to women's projects. A women's lobby group is presently working towards having the European Economic Community adopt such a policy *vis-à-vis* the North African countries.

Unless women can take their fate into their own hands, all attempts will ultimately be controlled by political powers which already use both culture and religion as weapons.

A sustained long-term effort is needed to give women both the political and the psychological means to use such international legal instruments. Social change comes slowly and such work does not result in a 'final product' for donors at the end of the year.

The difficulty in access to funding for women's networks must be noted as a major constraint to the WLUML. The underlying assumption seems to be that women's work should be for free. Although both donors and women are fighting this trend and requesting that the exchange value of women's work be recognized, anyone in contact with women networkers knows the degree of self-exploitation they are forced to accept for lack of funding; no male enterprise in the NGO landscape will ever be asked to make such sacrifices. Women lose their health in the process, as well as many aspects of their valued private lives. They burn out rapidly, and the turnover of coordinators and networkers is a clear indicator of the hardship they suffer.

Incidentally, fundraising, reporting and accounting for networking are time-consuming tasks which are never funded.

Then comes the question of 'project' versus long-sustained efforts towards social change. Projects can be limited in time and space; they have an end product which convinces donors that their money has been well spent. While international networks are not country-based, they need sustained funding for years in order to be effective. If they eventually have an end product to show, this only partially reflects their activities. They can elicit funds for meetings or publications but not for the lengthy months of prior work which lead to the successful outcome.

Coordination work, so obviously needed in a network like WLUML where 'networkers' are all over the world, is hard to fund: what it has to show for its achievements is of a qualitative rather than quantitative nature.

This leads to the question of evaluation and accountability of such networks. International networks are first and foremost accountable to the women they serve and self-evaluations should be acknowledged by donors as the fairest method. This leaves the problem of criteria, since no adequate terms of reference have been designed either by donor agencies or by the international networks themselves. New processes need to evolve and new instruments should be forged to allow for evaluations, in consultation with several women's networks and donors. Obviously a qualitative evaluation is a lot more difficult than a quantitative one, but in this case, it is the only valid instrument of measurement.

Finally, the language of management now in fashion among donor agencies is of great concern. I fear that increasingly only short-term, well-located projects showing glossy end-products will be funded, and that long-term efforts will be discarded because their results are more difficult to appreciate and/or demonstrate.

Rather than the language of aid or of management, I would advocate that we speak the language of solidarity. For if aid has only one direction – from funders to fundees – and implies no reciprocity, it fails to understand the interconnection of issues. Is it of no risk to the North that 'fundamentalism' develops not only in Muslim countries but in many others? Are not we, women from Muslim countries, on the frontline of something which is already affecting the countries of the North as well? Is it not of common benefit for Muslim women living in the North to learn to defend themselves against obscurantist versions of Islam? If WLUML is a South–South network, it also becomes a South–North network when it serves the needs of women from the North who, through their marriage or their children, suffer under Muslim laws. We cannot help but think that the erosion of reproductive rights in the US and in Western Europe is not without links to the rise of fundamentalism in the world.

Solidarity implies reciprocity: the recognition that what we do is also to the benefit of others, including those who presently fund our work. The artificial distinction between North and South, rich and poor, may very well be dismantled by the understanding of international solidarity in this reciprocal aspect. Women are hardly ever rich even in rich countries. The eligibility for funding is determined by irrelevant criteria which exclude women from Southern rich countries, or Western Europe, and leave them without financial means for their causes: it is as if all gender problems had been solved in those countries.

If women do not want to lose the rights they have acquired through long and sustained struggles, they must fully analyse the interconnection of obscurantist forces and draw the necessary conclusions.

NOTES

1 Women Living Under Muslim Laws, Aramon Plan of Action, April 1986, Montpelier France. This document was created at the founding meeting of the network.
2 This paragraph is taken from the Aramon Plan of Action document.
3 The following section on the objectives, past and ongoing collective projects of WLUML quotes extensively from Marie-Aimée Hélie-Lucas, Farida Shaheed and Faizun Zackariya, *Background and History of WLUML* (Montpelier, France 1991).
4 Quoted from Guidelines for Coordinators, Women and Law Program, WLUML internal document 1991.

5 The following examples are taken from the Guidelines for Coordinators, Women and Law Program.
6 Memorandum submitted to the Committee on Proposed Reforms to Muslim Personal Law, published June 1987 by MWRAF, 159 Kinsey Road, Colombo 8, Sri Lanka.
7 'Minimum Programs for Women', Muvman Liberasyon Fam, Lakaz Ros, Antelme Street, Forestside, Mauritius, 8 March 1987.

10
Canadian Women's Legal Fight for Equality

MARY EBERTS

Until the 1970s, the approach of resorting to legal action was not well known among Canadian feminists, although it has been used in a number of prominent cases in order to win, for example, rights for women to practise law in Canada. In a famous case back in 1930, Canadian women had won a declaration from the House of Lords in England that they were 'persons' under the Canadian constitution. But until the 1970s, most struggles for equality by Canadian women relied on difficult lobbying efforts, getting male parliamentarians, male administrators and male bureaucrats to accept the idea of equality, and slogging away at changing the Criminal Code. These were changes to decriminalize birth control, to give women a fair share of family property and to equalize women's ability to have custody of their children.

In the 1960s, the Royal Commission on the Status of Women was established in Canada. All the groups that had been lobbying so hard for equality through these years finally got the government to agree to a massive national study on the status of women. The 1970 report became a blueprint for what was going to happen over the next 15 years. It recommended sweeping reforms in the law and in government institutions. As a result, in the 1970s amendments to human rights codes were tabled in all jurisdictions in Canada to implement anti-discrimination measures of which women could take advantage. These measures also helped Canadian women to develop a legal culture, using lawyers to get governments to take action.

One of the reasons why human rights laws were so effective in this struggle was that the Supreme Court of Canada decided early on that human rights laws were clearly constitutional. They would take precedence over all other statutes, so they could be used even against government pension laws, government employment statutes, and so on. The law in Canada on sexual harassment, for example, was developed almost entirely in the area of the human rights codes. There were several landmark decisions both by tribunals under those codes and by the Supreme Court of Canada outlawing sexual harassment as a form of discrimination against women. Discrimination against pregnant women was also outlawed as a form of sexual harassment. Most recently, there have been several decisions using human rights codes to attack discrimination against gays and lesbians in employment and fringe benefits.

This move of using the human rights codes helped to create a matrix for the next significant development in Canadian women's fight for equality. That was the passage in 1981 of basic constitutional guarantees of equal rights for women in the Canadian Charter of Rights and Freedoms. Section 15 of the Charter, for example, guarantees equality before and under the law, while Section 28 states that all rights in the Charter should be extended equally to men and women. Women and visible minority groups, together with disabled people, gays and lesbians, had all participated in the development of the Charter's equality guarantees. This was the first time in Canadian history that grassroots, equality-seeking groups had been involved in the process by which governments agreed upon provisions of the constitution. It was a ground-breaking effort because all these groups then decided that they could not leave the working-out and implementation of those guarantees to litigators, governments and judges who were still mostly white Anglo-Saxon males. So there began to grow a number of advocacy groups to litigate under the Charter on behalf of women, gays and lesbians, disabled people, and visible and cultural minorities. These groups went into court either as interveners or by putting up some brave person as an individual plaintiff.

This litigation resulted in the articulation by the Supreme Court of Canada of the real substance of equality guarantees in our constitutional law. For example, the Supreme Court decided in 1989 that equality does not mean the same treatment, or formal equality. It recognizes that equality seekers and disadvantaged people are differently situated from mainstream individuals. As such, they are nonetheless entitled to claim equality and governments must adjust their programmes to accommodate these differences. We believe this was a landmark decision worldwide. Since then, the Supreme Court has made a number of strides in the articulation of equality for women and disadvantaged people. It has invalidated all the criminal prohibitions against abortion while supporting criminal prohibitions against violent pornography and hate propaganda, taking steps towards a stance very different from that held by the US Supreme Court.

One might think, with all that court action behind us, that Canadian feminists and disadvantaged people would be sitting pretty. Indeed, we are very proud of our achievements thus far. Funding the advocacy organizations to carry out this litigation has been a major task. The Women's Legal Education and Action Fund (LEAF), with which I am associated, must raise $600,000 every year to cover its litigation expenses. It has raised that money from ordinary women and men all over Canada through various events. We are also trying to raise an endowment to protect our funding against government interference because, after all these wonderful court victories, the government turned its attention to how these people were getting to court. They saw that this was the result of a programme they had set up in 1985 to offer a modest subsidy to people going to court to claim their equality. So they abolished it – they just cut it off completely in the February 1992 budget (see the following chapter by Andrée Côté on the Court Challenges Programme).

For the past two or three years, during the round of constitutional negotiations aimed at bringing the province of Quebec back into the mainstream of Confederation and adjusting certain other issues, women and other disadvantaged people have been almost totally excluded. So, even though the courts have declared our equality over and over again, and have recognized equality as an imperative of our constitutional law, the ability to take part in the formulation of that law at a political level has been denied to us. In particular, the Native Women's Association of Canada has run head-on into political repression. While several aboriginal groups have taken part in the constitutional negotiations and the principle of aboriginal self-government has finally been recognized, the Native Women's Association was refused permission when it asked to take part. It represents several thousand aboriginal women, many of whom live off reserves because they lost their Indian status when they married non-Indians; in turn, they have been excluded from the mainstream aboriginal groups because of their exclusion from the reserves. We finally won a decision recognizing the women's constitutional right to participate in discussions from the Federal Court of Appeal, and in August 1992 the Association asked for a seat at the table for the final meeting. But they got no response from the government, and the Charlottetown Agreement was concluded without them. Yet one of the elements in the Charlottetown Agreement was a declaration that the Canadian people have founded their government on respect for the rule of law.

So how well are Canadian women doing? On the one hand we have had fabulous court victories, and we have massive grassroots movements of Canadian women that pursue equality on a political basis and in the courts. Yet, when we get court decisions that recognize our equality aspirations within the framework of constitutional law, the government either cuts off the funding for future litigation or refuses to honour the decisions. The struggle for equality therefore remains on the agenda of Canadian women.

11
Canada Kills the Court Challenges Programme

ANDRÉE CÔTÉ

I would like to be able to say that Canada is living up to the international image that it projects, but unfortunately the Canadian government has just abolished one of the most important programmes for providing access to the courts for women and disadvantaged persons. This vital programme was instrumental in helping women from different communities – native women, disabled women, Afro-Canadian women, women from ethnic minorities, lesbians, young women and old women – to participate in the collective process of articulating a shared vision of equality that went far beyond the traditional formal equality espoused by legislators and the courts.

The courts have traditionally been the preserve of men. Men have occupied the benches and the legal profession, and they have used the courts to defend their position of power and privilege. And because of their dominant position, men have individually and collectively more access to the courts than women. This was clearly established in a thorough study by Gwen Brodsky and Shelagh Day of the court cases launched during the first three years of litigation under the equality provisions enshrined in Section 15 of the Canadian Charter of Rights and Liberties. In their study entitled *Canadian Charter Equality Rights for Women: One Step Forward or Two Steps Back?* they found that of the 600 cases initiated between 1985 and 1988, only seven had been launched by women and only four cases had been brought by national or ethnic minorities. The majority of cases were not about systemic discrimination but about such matters as drunk driving, marketing boards, regulation of airline landing fees and the manufacture of soft-drink cans. Equality rights provisions that had been enacted to redress the systemic discrimination against disadvantaged groups were, in fact, being used by men and by corporations to promote their interests and their power.

They also noticed that in a significant number of cases the equality guarantees enshrined in the Charter were actually being used to attack the interests of women. For example, the Nova Scotia Family Benefits Act, which provided benefits for single mothers but not single fathers, was being challenged as discriminatory on the basis of sex. There have also been many challenges brought, on the basis of the equality provisions in the Charter, against Criminal Code provisions that specifically recognized the gender dynamics of sexual abuse and provided special protection for women, such as the 'rape shield provision' that limited the circumstances in which questions could be asked of rape victims.

Judicial decision making results from a delicate operation of interpreting social reality in the light of legal rights and obligations, of balancing competing interests and defining the limits that can be ascribed to the exercise of these rights. Interpretation is contingent on perspective and, if women do not have access to the legal system to present a vision of the world that reflects the reality of their lives, the guarantees enshrined in the Charter run the risk of being perverted and, in effect, turned against us. In the first three years of the equality rights guarantee in the Charter, men were advancing a retrograde vision of equality, based on a formal notion of equality that would challenge any distinction on the basis of sex, such as the statute providing for family allowances to be paid to mothers.

Such a formal interpretation of equality rights distracted attention from the conditions of disadvantage suffered by women and jeopardized the few provisions that were actually beneficial to us. Despite the broad and generous provisions in the Charter, which are specifically framed to remedy restrictive interpretations of the past, women's equality rights guarantees were being hijacked by white, able-bodied rich men to defend their position of power and privilege. And the generally weak arguments articulated by the Attorney General clearly demonstrated that women could not count on the government to promote a vision of equality that would remedy our historical and systemic disadvantage. This is why equality-seeking groups across Canada fought so hard to make sure that women and other disadvantaged groups had a mechanism of accessing the justice system.

In 1985 the Court Challenges Programme was created. This programme funded test cases on equality rights and official minority language rights that had the potential of setting legal precedents of national importance. The programme provided up to $35,000 for test case litigation, and sometimes more when extraordinary funding was warranted. It was funded by the federal Department of Multiculturalism and Citizenship, with an annual budget of $2.75 million. The programme was accountable to the equality-seeking groups and official minority language rights organizations. Two panels, appointed after extensive community consultation, decided which cases were to be funded.

The programme has funded nearly 50 cases on sexual equality. For example, funding has been provided for a challenge being brought by an Inuit women's organization against discriminatory sentencing patterns detected when native women are victims of rape; a challenge to the Immigration Act over disallowing lesbian partners into the country has also been funded, as well as the case of women who are sponsored by their spouse and then lose their status on separation or divorce. The programme has funded many cases brought by native women who are trying to regain their rights to live on reserves after having been excluded by the Indian Act for many years.

In the programme's seven years, we have seen many important rulings decided upon by the Supreme Court of Canada. But the majority of the cases that the programme has funded are still at trial level. So we are just starting to explore the full scope and precise definition of equality rights in Canada. There have been major judicial victories but the programme brought more benefits than the strict legal victories. It helped women and persons from different communities, disabled persons, visible minorities, gays and lesbians, to get together in meetings of equality-seekers across the country where a common vision was starting to be developed, where common strategies were discussed. We were at a phase where work done specifically with women of different communities – immigrant women, disabled women, black women – was being developed.

The programme was terminated officially in February 1992, but it had been a slow process of abolition. In 1990 the programme was only renewed after an extensive battle fought by the equality-seeking groups and the official language minorities in Canada, and after a strong recommendation by the Standing Committee on Human Rights and the Status of Disabled Persons that it should be renewed to the year 2000. In renewing it, the government stipulated that it would no longer fund community meetings, education and public outreach. That was a clear move on the part of government to try to stop this growing movement.

The official reason given to justify the programme's termination in 1992 was budgetary restrictions. But it is hard to take the budgetary rationale seriously because, a few weeks after deciding that this vital programme had to be cut to save $2.75 million a year, the government announced that it was investing $4 billion in military helicopters. It was also said that the programme had achieved its purpose and that there was a sufficient body of case law that had been developed; but this was challenged by legal scholars and lawyers all over the country, including Madame Bertha Wilson, a former Justice of the Supreme Court. A final rationale offered by the government for the abolition of the Programme was that it was time to reinvest in the political process, and the courts should play their proper role and not deal with policy issues. This is probably one of the real reasons. We are witnessing an anti-Charter backlash in Canada. Just when women and other minority groups have the means and the expertise to access the courts, and are winning major victories, the government says that the courts have to play a more limited role and that women should address themselves to politicians and follow the traditional channel of the 'democratic' process.

The abolition of the Court Challenges Programme will be a very negative factor in the realization of our constitutional rights. If we cannot have access to the courts to enforce our rights, they become mere ideological discourse – propaganda. In effect, this will negatively affect the democratic development of Canada, since litigation is a check on governmental action and a means of ensuring that the government respects its Charter obligations.

All hope is not yet lost, however. The Standing Committee on Human Rights and the Status of Disabled Persons has held emergency hearings and come out with a strong report recommending the reinstatement of the programme. There has also been an enormous outcry from the legal profession, women's organizations, unions and human rights groups all over the country, challenging the government's decision.

If the programme does die in Canada, it should remain as a model that women and disadvantaged groups have in their memory bank for future reference. It is an interesting model for people who are working in other countries, or even at international level, for the recognition that women's rights are human rights.

EDITOR'S NOTE

In December 1992, the Canadian government announced it would not be reinstating the Court Challenges Programme. The Minister of Multiculturalism and Citizenship stated that the government had reviewed the report of the Standing Committee on Human Rights and the Status of Disabled Persons, which included a suggestion that the government seek other financial contributors to a future litigation support programme. The minister added:

> Consultations were initiated with the provinces to find funding partners. While interest was shown in the programme, only one province was prepared to discuss the development of a cooperative effort for funding Charter challenges with the federal government and other provinces. Furthermore, since the Standing Committee tabled its report, the Government has received over 2,000 representations. To date, no equality seeking group, language rights group, individual or association has indicated, to the Government, that they would wish to contribute to the funding of the Court Challenges Programme. Therefore, the Government has decided that it is unable to reinstate the Programme.

Canada's federal government first announced in its February 1992 budget that the Court Challenges Programme was terminated, along with 21 other agencies including the Law Reform Commission of Canada and the Economic Council of Canada, as part of a larger effort to reduce federal expenditures.

Part III
Mechanisms for Change

12

Beyond Borders: Women's Rights and the Issue of Sovereignty

KAREN KNOP

Much of the work on how to make international human rights law more responsive to women deals with one direction of responsiveness, namely from international law down. That approach looks at how the state can implement women's rights and how it can be held accountable for failure to do so, and it assumes the state's appropriateness as an actor both internationally and nationally.

There is another direction of responsiveness – from women up through the state to the international order and to the creation of international law and international human rights law. I will sketch in broad strokes three feminist approaches to the state as an international actor. These are not mutually exclusive but rather potentially complementary.

A first approach to the structures of international law is to insist on what Anja-Riitta Ketokoski has called 'parity democracy in international decision making'. This involves equal representation of gender-conscious women on all the international human rights bodies. We really need to be aware when there are vacancies on these bodies, to know who the candidates are and to lobby our governments in this respect. This approach assumes the potential for a 'feminization of power', and this is the phrase that Anja-Riita uses.

A second approach to the state as an actor, either internationally or nationally, is less optimistic. In her paper, 'To Bellow Like a Cow', Radhika Coomaraswamy says, 'If the state is entrusted with the responsibility of ensuring women's rights; if the state is always viewed as active and paternalistic in a benign manner, then this does pose serious questions. The nation-state in the Third World does not carry this "Scandinavian aura".'

This leads her to conclude that the future of human rights in South Asia does not lie with international treaties and states but with movements in civil society. She attributes social change to the coming together of the state and civil society at certain moments in time and space. She sees the role of civil society as mobilization and awareness, while the role of the state is articulation and implementation.

Taking Coomaraswamy's approach as a point of departure, then, women can strive to develop international civil society which is going to be a very heterogeneous combination of NGOs, independent experts and informal groups. These various configurations of women and men, experts and NGOs will serve to mobilize states to act internationally.

This, of course, suggests a number of things. First, we want to make all NGOs more gender-conscious. We want to strengthen women's NGOs, and increase their access to key international human rights bodies. We also want to organize groups of women publicists and women international lawyers.

The third approach to the state, a radical feminist approach, is to rethink the most fundamental concepts of international law – the ones that appear in the table of contents of international law textbooks, the ones that are always on diplomats' lips. There is a need for women to insert themselves into the international law discourse of sources, of process and of substance.

This may sound a little alarming. In speaking about the need to rethink the state, I am not suggesting we throw it out completely. Rather, I am suggesting asking some questions. When do women need the state on the international scene and when do they not? When does state sovereignty serve women's purposes, and when should they break down sovereignty to let their own voices be heard directly from within state boundaries and from across state boundaries?

Because international society is a group of states, feminist critiques of the state in the domestic context are relevant to international society. But we must keep in mind that the internal and external faces of the state are not identical. To quote from feminist writer Jean Bethke Elshtain: 'Historically, much of the power of the concept of sovereignty lay precisely in its encoding of the absolute, perpetual, indivisible power of a masculinized deity, a deity whose power was absolute and from everlasting to everlasting as a penultimate political form.'

So the image, as described by the writer, is of 'the sovereign self as an unproblematic, unified, sharply boundaried phenomenon.' Why not, these feminists ask, break down sovereignty? The issue has long been *who* should practise authority, but beyond this lie questions about *what* authority should be, and what it should look like. Kathleen Jones, another feminist writer, suggests: 'We can replace the voice of the sovereign master not with babble, but with efforts to recognize and admit responsibility for patterns of relationships that sovereign boundaries aim to negate.'

She is speaking at the domestic level, but I would argue that her analysis is relevant to international law. It is relevant because it questions our assumption that the sovereign state must act exclusively on behalf of its female population, that it must always represent us on the international scene. So when can the state simply not speak for women? Are there some cases when the state simply is not qualified to represent us or when we do not want it to represent us? This same question is already being asked by indigenous peoples in a different context. In fact, some native peoples who have some form of autonomy or self-government also have limited representation in certain international fora.

I will give one example of a case of breaking down sovereignty – the International Labour Organization (ILO). The International Labour Conference, which is equivalent to a general assembly, is where states, employers' organizations and workers come together to adopt conventions which deal with workers' rights; they also deal with human rights and women's rights. Its work is not as well-known as that of some UN bodies. At the ILO conference, each state is represented by four delegates: two from government, one from the employers' organizations, and one representing workers. Article 3(2) of the ILO constitution provides that when questions affecting women come before the conference, at least one of the two advisers permitted to delegates shall be a woman. But Article 3(6) goes on to say that advisers shall not speak except on a request made by the delegates whom they accompany and by the special authority of the president of the conference; and they may not vote. So a natural question flows from my analysis: why not provide for a woman to be the fifth delegate? Why not make the ILO quadripartite instead of tripartite?

These are a few thoughts on women's aspirations and how they might relate to state sovereignty. Some of them are very concrete and can be acted upon immediately. Some of the concerns are more theoretical and may involve further reaching changes. I hope that we can think in both these ways.

13

Do International Human Rights Laws Protect Women?

CECILIA MEDINA

One cannot answer this question without first acknowledging that it is difficult to separate promotional activities – those aimed at furthering the growth and development of human rights – from the protective ones, namely those aimed at supervising the observance of human rights by states. Protective measures play some sort of promotional role and usually more than a germ of protection can be traced in any promotional activity, for through promotion grows awareness, forming a sort of social control to discourage violations.

If we look at 'protection' in a broad sense, it could be said that international human rights laws have helped in the task of protecting women. Firstly, they have contributed to an awareness that women are also human beings and that, consequently, human rights are also their rights. This has been achieved primarily through the process of drafting international treaties concerning human rights for women. The existence of general international human rights law in itself has also helped by providing the legal foundation upon which women's struggle is based – that is, the principle of equality or non-discrimination. Standard-setting specifically aimed at women has been preceded by research and has been public, thereby placing the topic of women as holders of human rights, and the topic of the massive and systematic violation of these rights, in open fora.

The publicity surrounding these topics has not only helped to develop an awareness concerning human rights for women, but has also helped to legitimize women's struggle for the enjoyment of these rights. In this manner, international human rights laws, at both a regional and a universal level, have indeed helped in the preventive protection of these rights, convincing more and more individuals of the moral justification of helping women in their struggle and making some of them change their conduct accordingly. This is an ongoing process and, consequently, standard-setting in this area, or the further elaboration of the norms already established, is constantly helping to change in a positive way the general perception of women's struggle for full enjoyment of their rights.

Standard-setting fulfils yet another role in protecting women. When

78

international provisions come into force, obligations emerge for individual states. Even though international law has no compulsory power, the existence of international norms constitutes a strong incitement for states to comply and thus to create some form of mechanism at a national level to protect women against the violation of their human rights. In this sense, international human rights laws have also helped to protect women, although the help has been minuscule considering the magnitude of the problem.

A third form of protection – what one could call protection proper – is provided by setting up and making use of international mechanisms for the purpose of protecting women against the violation of their human rights. From this viewpoint, the answer to the question posed at the start of this paper – do international human rights laws protect women? – would probably have to be a robust 'no'. International human rights laws in general, and inter-American human rights laws in particular, have not protected women against the violation of their rights. There are reasons for this.

Given a body of international law based upon the principle of non-discrimination and a decent catalogue of human rights, the effectiveness of international mechanisms to protect human rights in general depends heavily upon two factors: one is the stand the international supervisory organ takes with regard to these rights, and the other is the attitude of the potential users towards the mechanisms. Addressing the first factor, the element that makes the difference is the composition of the international organ. If it is composed of people who look positively and imaginatively at the subject matter which they have to protect, there will be advancement. A clear example is the history of the Inter-American Commission on Human Rights; established as a study group, it developed into an active defender of human rights and created a procedure to deal with human rights violations.[1]

Thus, an important task in making international human rights laws work for women is involvement in the selection of the members of relevant international organs. It is important that the United Nations Committee on Human Rights, the European Commission and Court of Human Rights, and the Inter-American Commission and Court of Human Rights be composed of individuals who roughly represent the gender composition of member states, and it is as important that those who accede to these organs, be they men or women, have a positive attitude towards equality of the sexes. We cannot close our eyes to the fact that the values cherished by individuals influence their decisions; if the members of a supervisory body have not accepted the value of equality of the sexes, if this is not heartfelt, they will tend not to include women and their problems in the range of their supervisory powers. The only way to counterbalance any inclination to ignore women as holders of human rights is by actions undertaken by the other factor mentioned above, the users of the system – in this case, women themselves.

No supervisory system, national or international, will work without individuals believing in it and making use of it on a regular basis. It is essential that users learn about the existence of the system, know about its possibilities and are in a position to use it without great sacrifice. Taking Latin America as an example, most women have no knowledge of the United Nations or the inter-American system – and the few who do, do not visualize the system for the promotion and protection of human rights as an instrument to be used for their particular problems. International laws and international organizations are considered alien, to be at best ignored and at worst distrusted. The task here is to educate women about the system. This means not only teaching them about its existence and possibilities; it also means making women realize that they have to act in the more general context of human rights, and that it is to their benefit to have violations considered by supervisory organs in the realm of general human rights.

In Latin America, there is a second obstacle to be overcome. Belief is widespread that international human rights law is meant for what are called 'gross' violations; in Latin American terms, these would include disappearances, summary executions, torture and prolonged and arbitrary detention. In the face of these horrors, the national communities, including women, find it difficult to resort to the system to complain about what might be considered 'minor' problems. There are obviously misconceptions about the magnitude of women's rights violations and about the role international human rights law should play, and these misconceptions must be corrected. Again education is needed, along with research. The magnitude, in human terms, of the violation of women's human rights has to be demonstrated to dissipate women's fears that they are being unreasonably demanding.

Women's education cannot be undertaken in a traditional way through formal lecturing. The task is wider than just international human rights laws, so ways should be found to integrate human rights teaching with other activities. Great numbers of women have been able to develop within the framework of 'popular movements', formed to deal with survival problems such as the need for food, shelter and medical care. One example is a project in Chile where women, with the help of architects and planners, have built their own houses. Besides learning the basic skills needed to put up walls and install water and electricity, women had to negotiate credit with banks, make budgets and so forth, thereby acquiring a self-confidence in matters of the world. Another example, also in Chile but some years ago, occurred when women organized themselves to counterbalance the destabilization campaign instigated by the United States government to overthrow President Allende. Women set up a system to distribute scarce food to households, learning in the process how to operate in the financial world and how to do it with a social-justice approach. The groups involved in these activities would be ideal subjects for human rights education. But financing would, of course, have to be found.

The system also has to be made accessible to women. To this end, two actions are needed. The first involves the international supervisory organs which must become really 'public'. International organizations are usually not within easy reach of individuals; in many countries of Latin America, Asia and Africa, they are not even within easy reach of lawyers. It is vitally important that the United Nations and the Organization of American States, to name those relevant to Latin America, disseminate information. Local libraries should also keep records of the activities of these organizations, so that precedents can be used to further the universalization of the scope of human rights. These activities could be undertaken by international governmental organizations and by private institutions.

Private institutions also have vitally important roles to play in the second action needed to make the system accessible to women. It would be a tremendous help if local non-governmental organizations could be established with a body of well-trained lawyers to represent women in local courts and defend them with arguments based on international human rights laws. These organizations should obviously be connected to others working where international supervisory organs are located, so that a fruitful interaction can develop between national and international progress.

These suggestions are only a few of the things that should be done to make this world a better place to live, a world where we can coexist with fairness for everybody. We can only hope that at least some of them are realized soon.

NOTE

1   For information on this, see C. Medina, *The Battle of Human Rights. Gross, Systematic Violations and the Inter-American System* (Martinus Nijhoff, Dordrecht, The Netherlands, 1988) Chapter IV, pp. 67–92.

14

Holding Governments Accountable by Public Pressure

DOROTHY Q. THOMAS

International human rights advocacy is just one of many strategies available to influence and pressure governments to be more accountable to women. Non-governmental women's rights institutions and activists use radio and other media, grassroots communities' activism, popular education, legal literacy, development work and many other strategies to promote and secure women's basic human dignity.

Such activism on behalf of women in the non-governmental community not only happens in different ways but at different levels – from the street all the way to the Cabinet – in local, national and international spheres. For example, the efforts of a small community of women in Brazil to end police indifference to domestic violence bred a national movement to protest the state's failure to prosecute such abuse; it led eventually to condemnation by the international community of Brazil's flouting of its international obligations to guarantee women equality before, and equal protection under, the law.

However, until recently, this kind of effective use of the human rights strategy with regard to women's rights was extremely rare. We now have an opportunity to use it to a much greater degree, particularly if women have input into the way it is used. This is an emerging and dynamic field.

What is Human Rights Watch?

Human Rights Watch is made up of five regional Watch Committees: Africa Watch, Asia Watch, Middle East Watch, Americas Watch and Helsinki Watch. These regionally oriented human rights organizations are united under one umbrella organization: Human Rights Watch. There are also four thematic or cross-regional projects: on arms transfers to abusers of human rights, on freedom of expression issues, on prison conditions, and on women.

The Women's Rights Project was established in 1990 to work in conjunction with the five regional Watch Committees to monitor violence against women and discrimination on the basis of gender worldwide. It grew out of Human Rights Watch's recognition of the epidemic proportions of violence against women and gender-discrimination, and of the past failure of human rights organizations to hold governments accountable for either committing or tolerating abuses of women's basic human rights.

In the US, we are trying to determine the issue that would make the most effective contribution, because there are many groups doing work on various aspects of violence against women and sex discrimination. We have to decide whether to do work on rape or on access of immigrant women to justice in domestic violence cases, or whether we should do an analysis on the limitations of US refugee law with regard to women seeking asylum from other countries. We have done work in Poland, in Czechoslovakia and will continue to do work in Eastern Europe.

The government officials we deal with most consistently have not previously been questioned on issues of abuse of women's rights, so we are hoping this question will be integrated more thoroughly into the issue of the human rights performance of governments.

What Does It Mean to Use a Human Rights Methodology?

To use a human rights approach to influence governments with regard to women's human rights requires a thorough grounding in current human rights methodology, aptly summed up by Diane Orentlicher (*Harvard Human Rights Journal*, 1990) as 'promoting change by reporting facts'. In essence, holding governments accountable for abuses of human rights requires NGOs to: (a) carefully document alleged abuses; (b) clearly demonstrate state accountability for those abuses under international law; and (c) develop a mechanism for effectively exposing documented abuse nationally and internationally.

This method, as Orentlicher notes, has been subjected to intense scrutiny, particularly by governments concerned about the costs of being labelled violators of human rights. From the early days of the international human rights movement, organizations like Amnesty International and Human Rights Watch were criticized by governments whose records were being examined, and the credibility of their human rights reporting was challenged. Orentlicher notes:

> during the first term of the Reagan Administration in particular, the public battle over facts between the Administration and the human rights community were heated, harsh and at times downright nasty.

Reflecting on this history of the human rights method is important to women's rights advocacy for at least two reasons. First, it points out that even before women's rights enter into the debate, human rights work is extremely controversial. Second, and more pressing for NGOs seeking to use the human rights methodology on behalf of women, it highlights the degree to which the credibility of their fact-finding is of paramount consideration.

The Women's Rights Project's primary purpose is to apply this methodology to abuses of women's human rights, in collaboration with women's and human rights groups all over the world. The aim is to press governments to adhere to their international obligations to protect the rights of all people without regard to distinction of any kind, including sex.

Governments do not at all appear to enjoy the prospect of being held accountable under international law for their treatment of women. It took the United States government until 1989 to include violence against women, sex discrimination and other violations in its annual country reports on human rights practices; no doubt this was in part because of a reluctance to have its own record examined. The first non-US official with whom the project met to discuss his government's tolerance of women's rights abuses responded that it was none of our business and, in any case, *his* wife was happy.

The kind of reactions we get in doing this work tells us a lot about what we are up against. Most governments do not expect to be asked about women's rights, are not prepared to answer questions about women's human rights and, when pressed, officials will allude to their wife's happiness or, in essence, duck the issue. However, the level of pressure we can put on governments in this manner is clearly very high, and we have an enormous amount of work to do.

Women everywhere are discovering that the human rights method, with its universal language, moral authority and measure of accountability, provides a useful tool for invigorating local struggles and putting additional pressure on governments to end state-sponsored or tolerated abuse of women. Using the international human rights framework has also reinforced the understanding of particular issues for many activists: for example, violence against women is a cross-cultural phenomenon, as well as having culturally specific forms.

In the short time that the Women's Rights Project of Human Rights Watch has been in existence, we have had the opportunity to work with women's groups in, among other places, Poland, Kuwait, Brazil, Pakistan, Peru and Czechoslovakia. In all these countries, women are to a greater or lesser degree adopting the human rights method to expose government commission of, or complicity in, abuses of women's human rights. In Brazil, the women's movement has launched a national campaign promoting women's rights as human rights (Os Direitos Da Mulher Sao Direitos Humanos). In Pakistan, women's rights are at the heart of the human rights struggle, and activists have vigorously challenged statutory discrimination and state-sponsored violence against women as abuses of human rights. In Peru, women's rights and human rights activists are beginning to band together to combat abuses by both parties in the conflict there, including abuses of women's human rights.

The first Women's Rights Project report that used the human rights method to hold a government accountable was issued by Americas Watch. Focusing on domestic violence in Brazil, it was the first time that a human rights organization had ever looked at the question of violence against women in the home as an abuse of human rights. It represented a strong collaborative effort with the women's rights movement in Brazil, which had been advocating for many years the ending of Brazilian courts' acceptance of 'legitimate defence of honour', used to acquit men who kill their allegedly unfaithful wives. We also looked at the state's systematic failure to punish other crimes of violence against women in the home, including battery and rape.

The report, published in both English and Portuguese, struck a chord in Brazil. It demonstrated that the state was responsible for something previously rejected as a private issue, beyond the scope of the state's responsibility, and that governments had an obligation both to protect women and to punish such abuse. It also provided an opportunity for women's rights and human rights organizations to work together both locally and internationally. There was very close cooperation with the local women's rights groups, in conceptualizing the issues as well as in identifying the vulnerable women and determining exactly where reforms were needed. This collaboration contributed to the enormous press attention given to the report, both in Brazil and elsewhere, and to the impact of its recommendations.

It is important that work is a joint enterprise with local women's rights groups. The local groups must want to do the work and feel that it won't backfire on them. The benefits are that the report speaks a language that is relevant, and represents another level of pressure from an international agency that is not seen to be implicated in local politics – the report is seen as having been done by an independent agency from outside the country.

We also worked very closely with women's rights organizations in Pakistan to determine the most effective and sensitive way to raise the issue of violence against women in custody. Dealing with cultural, religious or any justification for an abuse of women's human rights usually calls for a complicated analysis of the situation with careful attention paid to the particular context in which the abuse occurs. In Pakistan we made a very clear analysis of discriminatory laws: the state claimed these were Islamic, although they were subject to an enormous amount of interpretation internally. We denounced the laws as a clear violation of international human rights.

Out of these and other extremely positive developments in the emerging field of international women's human rights, several serious practical problems have emerged. As noted earlier, the reason that the human rights methodology has been effective in exposing abuse, and raising government accountability for human rights violations in general, rests on three factors:

1. the facts are indisputable and well-documented;

2. a consensus exists that the documented practices constitute abuses for which a government can rightfully be held accountable under international law;

3. some working mechanism exists to expose the abuse and bring the requisite local and international pressure to bear.

Although in doing international women's human rights work we have found that one or even two of these minimal conditions exist, in our experience all three are rarely present and, in general, none are. This poses a serious and pressing practical impediment to the effective use of the human rights method to influence governments with regard to the rights of women.

GETTING THE FACTS

The problem is not that the facts do not exist. The problem is getting the facts. And that is a problem that relates to resources, both human and material. If you are a women's rights activist in the world today, when you stick your head up and say 'I'm for women', you are likely to get it shot off, either literally or figuratively. Women's rights work is, by its very nature, a political struggle; it challenges the fundamental structure of society. For that reason, it is often restricted or prohibited altogether, and women who engage in it often lack support and are frequently at risk.

For example, the Egyptian government recently closed down the Egypt-based Arab Women's Solidarity Association, a group known for its advocacy of women's rights in the Arab world. In Poland, a woman's rights organization was denied the right to register officially on the grounds that, according to the judge, who happened to be a woman, 'women in Poland have too many rights and need to rest.' In other places, the restrictions on women's activism may be less blatant, but no less effective. A Brazilian women's rights activist told us: 'It is possible that I, as an outspoken feminist, could be murdered here. Only the women's movement would try to protect me.'

By and large, women's groups and activists have neither the time nor the resources to disengage from the broader political struggle and devote themselves to gathering facts. Meanwhile, those organizations that have the human and material resources to document abuse – the local and international human rights organizations – do *not* focus on abuses of women's human rights. This information gap is a very serious problem for the emerging field of women's human rights. In the absence of sound documentation, women's human rights work will not stand up under scrutiny and, thus, its effectiveness may be compromised. Support is needed for both women's and human rights groups to do this documentary work so that the two can work together, train each other and exchange information.

BUILDING CONSENSUS

Even if women's and human rights groups do manage to get the resources to do documentary work and to publicize prevailing abuses, there is still no consensus that the practices being documented will be seen as human rights abuses for which governments can be held accountable under international law.

Anyone who has worked on domestic violence knows that it constitutes an abuse which governments must protect against and punish and for which states ought to be held accountable. Yet, it has rarely been viewed in this way by international human rights practice. A government should be held accountable not only for what it commits but for what it fails to do – in this case, for failing to provide women with equal protection before the law. This is an extremely important evolution in the thinking of Human Rights Watch and it enables us to do relevant women's rights' work.

Similarly rape, although it is often used by government agents to punish, intimidate or coerce female victims, has only recently begun to be viewed as a form of torture rather than solely as a form of cruel and inhuman punishment or strictly as a violent sexual act. Thus, while we may assert that certain abuses of women's rights constitute abuses of human rights, a popular consensus on this has yet to emerge. It does not even exist within the narrower confines of the human rights community.

Thus, those of us seeking to use the human rights methodology must realize that if we are going to take on this strategy, we need to build this consensus. If it is left to the human rights community alone, it will not happen. The women's rights and human rights groups need to work together. And they need support.

CREATING A MECHANISM

The final necessary component of using the human rights strategy to hold governments accountable to women is the need to develop mechanisms for exposing well-documented abuses of women's human rights. This is an area in which we again encounter problems. Our networks, both at the local and at the international level, are inadequate. In almost every country I visit, the human rights and women's rights organizations do not communicate or, worse, are antagonistic. This same problem exists between the local organizations and the international ones. Education is necessary: people need to know how the human rights organizations work and international human rights organizations also need to be educated. This exchange is extremely important in building an effective mechanism for denouncing abuses of women's human rights. If we do not link hands, we will not make change.

In conclusion, I want to stress that the facts do exist. The consensus will emerge. And we will develop mechanisms for exposing abuse and for holding governments accountable for it. However, to do so, we will need the support of the donor community.

15

Barriers to Funding for Women's Legal Rights: Some Critical Issues for Consideration by the North

SHANTHI DAIRIAM

Equal rights for women is about the dismantling of male privilege, institutionalized not only through laws but also through social conventions and norms. This dismantling process cannot take place without the agency of women's constituencies. Women's groups and organizations need donor support in building up the agency of women, even though this may present difficulties from the point of view of established funding procedures. Much larger allocations of resources must be made for working with women than is currently the practice.

Since 1975, development for women has been promoted through many initiatives internationally, regionally and nationally. There have been levels of gain for women in some parts of the world, primarily in areas such as life expectancy, health and employment. But, in comparison with men, there has been no real change with regard to the redistribution of resources, nor has there been a shift in values placed on men and women. Male preference within the family and at the public level is still the norm (Staudt 1989).

The mechanisms and institutions created to promote the development of women at national and international levels have been less than effective for various reasons – the bureaucratic nature of the organizations concerned, inadequate allocation of resources, their location in inconsequential units of the overall development machinery (or their separateness and consequent ghettoization), and at times their being staffed by people whose attitudes reinforced the subordination of women.

So the question still remains: how do we bring about redistributive justice? It is becoming increasingly clear that many of the initiatives have not altered the balance of power because there was no understanding that redistributive justice meant just that – an alteration in the balance of power and a dismantling of male privilege. As a result, development has been planned for women, resulting in value-loaded forms of intervention which have accepted male superiority. Conceptual biases that have distorted the reality of women's lives, their interests and their needs have further compounded the problem. What is needed is the space for, and the recognition of, women's collective voice in determining development goals for women through 'the agency of women'. This could be defined as a constituency of women capable of recognizing what is in their interests and having the capacity to hold bureaucracies accountable for creating the conditions necessary for dismantling the structures of their subordination.

Hitherto development initiatives for women have provided inputs to mitigate lower levels of education, health, employment, etc. But not enough attention has been paid to the complex social, legal and political structures that created and perpetuated these deficiencies. Even less attention has been paid to the importance of removing these structures through the agency of women.

Some examples from Malaysia illustrate this point. Women's organizations there have been engaged in a great deal of advocacy work for equal rights within the past 20 years. The experiences and outcome of such advocacy has been variable. For example, a uniform civil code for family laws relating to non-Muslims, seen as critical in the multiracial context of Malaysia, took 13 years for implementation from the time the advocacy was initiated. Legislated in Parliament in 1976, seven years after the advocacy work started, the code was not implemented until 1982.

I personally think that this was such an uphill struggle because it challenged institutionalized male privilege (the code, among other things, abolished polygamy for non-Muslims) and because the bureaucracies responsible for implementation were not accountable to women. There was no visible constituency of women making this demand – only a small group of women tenaciously badgering the powers that be and gaining access to them through their social and political contacts. Currently there are problems of implementation with this code. Cultural imperatives are surfacing ten years after implementation, and demands are being made to change rules to accommodate cultural needs. Other implementation problems seem to be arising out of the need to satisfy bureaucratic conveniences.

Rape laws were amended in 1989, imposing more stringent punitive measures that would act as a deterrent. Medical and police procedures were also changed to ensure more humane treatment of the rape survivor. In spite of such reforms, we hear of very few cases of women reporting rape. In some areas where male power and privilege is firmly entrenched, reform has not yet been possible; these include discriminatory laws pertaining to inheritance, citizenship, guardianship of children and income tax.

Elson (1991) helps us to understand such barriers to the attainment of equal rights for women when she says that rights have to be examined in the context of socially conferred capability to exercise those rights. Women may theoretically have equal rights, but they may not have the social right to exercise them. For example, we have to question whether women are able to make choices as autonomous beings regarding their health, their employment, use of their income and family resources, their inheritance or their participation in public life. When women collude with cultural imperatives which place a premium on cultural identity at the expense of their rights within the family, or when women who have been violated by the crime of rape dare not seek redress, it indicates that they are conforming to a social convention which demands such behaviour. Resisting it could mean having to face trade-offs such as loss of social respectability, of emotional support or kinship support, which these women need to mediate their access to resources for survival. When women are not in a position to cope with such trade-offs, it indicates a lack of social and political capability to exercise their rights.

We need to ask, therefore, in each area of rights – what are women's capabilities and how do these compare with those of men? If women enjoy fewer capabilities, there is male bias in the social order. Sen (1990) states that 'acute inequalities happen because the underdog has accepted the legitimacy of the unequal social order.' Where women are concerned, this translates into accepting the overwhelming superiority of men in a way which colours and delegitimizes the perception of their interests, needs and contributions. It is therefore critical that the agency of women, through which women's perceptions of what is legitimate is transformed, and women themselves provide the leverage to transform the prevailing social order.

Who will work towards the creation of the agency of women? The task is complex and difficult, the process long and drawn-out. In Malaysia, women's groups now need to move from being advocates of equal rights to creating the constituencies and the agency of women. What is now needed is support for constituency building. This may pose difficulties. There is no visible product. What is involved is a process of mobilizing women that will not lend itself to being monitored according to bureaucratic requirements of time frame, inputs and quantifiable outputs.

Women will come to the scene with different levels of consciousness and social capability. While the mobilization needs to take place in the specific context of health, nutrition, education, economic or reproductive rights or women's rights within the family, the goal will have to be the creation of a constituency of women who have the capability to exercise these rights. A great deal of importance will have to be attached to the processes through which a particular issue, such as provision of employment opportunities or even meeting basic nutritional needs, is addressed. These activities should provide the opportunity for women to come together, to share experiences, to understand the social and political structures that have been the cause of their malnutrition or unemployment, and to participate in planning their development. Through this process women should be able to provide support for one another and gain the collective strength needed to challenge oppressive gender and class relations. These processes should also recognize women's right to gain control of the direction the project itself should take and make provisions for that. There needs to be flexibility of approach and an orientation towards the critical importance of the process, and not just the visible product.

Existing women's organizations need to be strengthened if they are to work towards constituency building. Their good intentions and commitment cannot carry them through. They need skills development and an expansion of their staff resources – another area of difficulty for donors. While funds may be available for project work, hardly any is available, in my experience, for staffing. One of the reasons why Malaysian women's groups cannot go beyond advocacy work is because they do not have the capability for constituency building in terms of human resources and time. Some women are already doing three jobs – one that receives a salary and two that do not. One has had to make unjustifiable personal sacrifices to make this possible. In my personal opinion, there is gross unfairness in the distribution of resources at the international donor agency level. One has seen donor agency consultants drawing huge fees for various kinds of work while the development of women has to be done for nothing.

A further problem for donors is that they need to see funds going to the poorest countries. But male domination and female subordination and resistance to change exists globally, albeit in differing forms. Furthermore these structures of subordination are not contained locally. There are such cross-cutting influences as the international economic order and world trade which impinge negatively on women in various corners of the world. If male privilege is to be dismantled through the agency of women, work needs to be done nationally, regionally and internationally. Support is needed for work at all levels, and in countries that are not seen as deserving assistance. To divide the movement according to the distinction of resource-poor countries does not help.

In the final analysis, we cannot avoid the question of a much larger allocation of resources to women's work than is currently the norm. In many UN agencies, 3.5 per cent of projects benefit women, representing 0.2 per cent of budget allocations. Less than one per cent of FAO projects contain strategies to reach women. The US$5 million budget of UNIFEM is a drop in the bucket of its host, the US$700 million UN Development Programme.[1] Our first struggle has to be towards securing the volume of resources we need, with this directed towards the kind of work that has to be done to create a political force of women.

NOTE

1 These are figures taken from Staudt (1989). They are not current figures and the sums of money indicated have increased in absolute terms. There is, however, no change proportionally to the money allocated for women's projects.

16

Women, Development and Justice: Using the International Convention on Women's Rights

MARSHA A. FREEMAN

The Convention on the Elimination of All Forms of Discrimination Against Women (CEDAW) is a powerful instrument for the delivery of development with justice. As an international legal instrument, the CEDAW states the basic international standards of equality in the law and before the law, to which all countries must at least aspire if they do not yet adhere. As a development policy document, it requires accountability from governments for their actions to advance women's legal, economic, and social status. Above all, it provides guidelines for legal, policy and programme development to promote equality as a means to justice.

What is meant by justice is found within the language of the convention itself. The basic premise of the convention is that women have a right to the full enjoyment of human rights and fundamental freedoms 'on a basis of equality with men', and most of the articles are framed in the context of equality. But the convention does not stop with an aspiration to formal equality; rather, it promotes positive action to eliminate the barriers that keep women from succeeding even where opportunity appears to be equal. Article 4 provides for temporary special measures to accelerate *de facto* equality, with the objective of equal opportunity and treatment. Most importantly, Article 5 provides for action to modify custom and eliminate prejudice and stereotyping – the assumptions and commonplace actions that reinforce women's inferiority and stall progress.

The examination of custom, the elimination of prejudice, and the development of measures to promote equality in practice as well as in law, are the tools of justice. The convention obligates governments to change not only law but culture. It indicates clearly that women are entitled to a fair share of society's benefits to balance the enormous productive and reproductive responsibilities they carry. It requires governments to address the injustice and oppression visited on the female half of humanity solely because they are female. It establishes that women's rights are human rights.

The Convention as a Human Rights Instrument

The rights articulated in the CEDAW are simply the rights all humans should be accorded under the standards of the Universal Declaration of Human Rights and other major international human rights instruments[1] – stated in prescriptive terms that indicate the issues nation-states must address if women are to enjoy the human rights that the world has come to accept as basic. In the context of civil and political rights, this means that governments must exert themselves to ensure that social and legal barriers are removed so that women can attend meetings, write for publication, and run for office as well as vote.[2] In the context of economic, cultural and social rights – the positive rights that require significant state action to deliver – this means that governments must ensure that whatever they can provide to their citizens, they provide fully to women as well as to men. It means that governments must regulate private as well as public acts, to prevent discrimination 'by any person, organization or enterprise'.[3] And in the context of fundamental freedoms, it means in particular that governments must establish an ethic of freedom that includes protection of women's personal security and freedom of movement in the streets and in the home.[4]

Enforcement of the convention, like enforcement of any human rights instrument, is a question of political will and organization. What differentiates it from other human rights instruments is the extent to which enforcement depends on political will and organization at the national level. This is true for two reasons: the nature of the convention's own enforcement mechanisms, and the nature of the rights articulated in it.

As many analysts have pointed out,[5] enforcement of the convention at the international level consists only of a reporting procedure in which the Committee on the Elimination of Discrimination Against Women (CEDAW) reviews country reports on the status of women and engages in 'constructive dialogue' with representatives of reporting countries.[6] The convention does not include a complaint procedure or provision for investigating violations and does not provide for formal NGO input at the international level. This places a premium on national level action by an active citizenry, including non-governmental organizations, to articulate and press for enactment of laws and policies that meet the convention's standards.[7] It also places a premium on NGO involvement in or monitoring of report preparation at the national level to call attention to the convention's importance, as well as NGO monitoring of the review process to provide information about the CEDAW's response to the country report.

National level action on convention implementation is also critical because enforcement of women's human rights presents a special set of issues that must be resolved largely on the national level. This convention is about women as citizens and as a special category of citizen. The rights articulated in it go to the heart of personal and family relationships as no other human rights instrument does. To state, for example, that women shall have 'the same rights and responsibilities [as men] during marriage and at its dissolution' (Article 16(c)), or that women shall have equal legal capacity with men (Article 15), is to challenge the assumptions, laws, and customs under which millions of people live.[8] As Unity Dow of Botswana has found, challenging inequality in nationality laws (Article 9), for example, can call forth the full force of the state to support discrimination in the name of preserving the culture.[9]

It is possible to address the issue of culture at the international level. The articulation of universal norms by the CEDAW is the essence of that effort. Global awareness campaigns, and internationally organized 'alerts' on particular issues or particular cases concerning women's human rights, put governments on notice that egregious violations of women's human rights will be noticed just as disappearances and political oppression are.[10] But as a practical matter, the human rights issues involving women, because they are so meshed with issues of culture, are resolved largely at the country level. Cultures change because people change and make demands on their culture. Women and men who understand the universality of human rights – who understand injustice – change the culture from within. It is incumbent on us as international activists and as donors to be creative in supporting those efforts.

The Convention as a Legal Document

The convention is the only document to have emerged from the International Decade for Women that carries legal obligations. Despite the difficulties of enforcement, much of the convention's significance lies in its statement of international legal obligations to undertake major changes in law and policy to provide for equality and deliver justice.

The convention's principles stand as a bill of rights for women. Its language is quite general – though no more general than that of any other human rights instrument – and each country must determine the nature of enforcement within its particular legal and administrative system. That means that every country must undertake a close examination of its laws and regulatory policies to determine where changes should be made in accordance with convention principles.

In many countries the most difficult part of this examination will concern Articles 15 (legal capacity) and 16 (family law). Governments that readily subscribe to principles of equality in employment (Article 11) or education (Article 10) may balk at dealing with issues of family relations and property in the light of the convention.[11] Implementation of these articles requires an examination of relationships between men and women, between family members, and between family and state, that affects every citizen personally as well as theoretically. In countries with multiple or religious legal systems, in which personal status issues (usually marriage, divorce, inheritance, adoption and burial) are governed by custom or religious law, governments may refuse to 'interfere' with personal status laws on grounds of preserving local culture and ethnic or religious identity. This attitude can be the result of a variety of motives ranging from historical prejudices to political judgment, to lack of resources, to sheer lack of imagination.

It is therefore important to support studies and educational activities by non-governmental groups that are in a position to articulate the local issues and make recommendations on implementing the convention in local legal systems. The most recent successful example of this is a study by the Women and Law in Southern Africa Research Project (WLSA),[12] produced in August 1992, which examined customary law in Eastern and Southern Africa in light of the equality requirements of convention Article 16. The WLSA study concluded that 'international women's rights norms are not incompatible with African customary law'[13] and made recommendations for application of Article 16 in African legal systems that reflect this view.

As an international treaty, the convention is usable in different ways in different legal systems. In some systems, it may be self-executing;[14] that is, it becomes the law of the land upon ratification or accession. In most common law systems, it is not self-executing, but states the general premises upon which laws and policies should be examined and changed to promote equality. According to a number of eminent common law jurists, international human rights norms can and should be used in common law systems to interpret laws and constitutions.[15]

Ratification of the CEDAW does not mean that the law will suddenly become the single most useful tool to achieve justice, particularly as the law has its limits. Even in states with highly developed equality laws, enforcement can be difficult and expensive and frequently stumbles over cultural barriers. Studies of gender in the courts in the US have shown consistently that interpretation and application of the law, which rests on the perspective of individual judges and court personnel, is far from fair to women.[16] In every country, court procedures are intimidating;[17] some systems are so paralyzed by caseload and procedural limitations that remedies remain a phantom hope.[18] But law can be an expression of a culture's aspirations as well as its limitations. Certainly, equality will not be achieved without stating it, through the law, as a public goal.

The importance of confirming equality as a public goal through law is that it gives women choices. Having the right to enter waged employment on a pay and promotion scale equal to those of men does not mean that all women will do it, but it raises the possibility for women to improve their economic position. Having the right to obtain a divorce on the same grounds as one's husband does not mean that a woman will immediately leave the marriage, but it does shift the balance of power between spouses. Having the right to decide how many children to have does not mean that women will all decide to stop having children, but it gives women the ability to plan their lives and provide more effectively for their children. Even given cultural and economic constraints, having rights means having options. It gives women the ability to dream a different reality.[19]

CEDAW is not the last word in legal development to promote justice for women. It is the first. It remains for groups and individuals, for scholars, lawyers and activists, for government officials and for donors, to bring it alive within legal systems. The means vary by system, but the effort must be universal.

The Convention as a Development Document

The convention is a blueprint for development with justice. It was framed to establish women's rights in the development context, reflecting a recognition that development could not be successful without women's full participation and acknowledgement of their rights.

The resolution authorizing the drafting of the convention's first incarnation, the Declaration on the Elimination of All Forms of Discrimination Against Women, was sponsored almost entirely by developing countries.[20] The preamble to the Declaration, and ultimately to the convention, asserted that discrimination against women is an affront to human dignity and 'is an obstacle to the participation of women, on equal terms with men, in the political, social, economic and cultural life of their countries, hampers the growth of the prosperity of society' and impedes development. The UN General Assembly that approved the convention in 1979, not long after organization of the G-77 as a voting bloc, was dominated in numbers by developing countries.[21] The convention clearly stands as an acknowledgement that elimination of discrimination against women is a universal value and is critical to development.

The meaning of the convention as a development document is tied closely to its meaning as an elucidation of women's human rights. The essence of the issue, and of the convention, is that women cannot effectively participate in development unless their human capacity is fully recognized in law and in fact, and countries cannot develop successfully unless women participate effectively in their society as fully recognized adults. This means that women must be seen as individuals capable of making decisions that are good for themselves, their families and their societies.

Women's decision-making ability at the family level has been well documented. Indeed, the rising proportion of female-headed households in every region of the world[22] indicates that women are, by necessity, making decisions every day about money, work (including running farms), where to live, how to educate themselves and their children, and whether to have more children. Educated women hold professional, business, and government positions everywhere in the world, even in countries in which most women are extremely poor and oppressed. Any argument that women are, by their nature, incapable of thinking carefully and making important decisions flies in the face of reality.

The convention provides an outline of the realities of development as it relates to women. It suggests a programme of action for governments, citizens and NGOs to implement women's rights as basic to development. Education, health care, employment, participation in public decisions, property ownership, and planned families enable women to reach their potential as individuals and as members of families and of society.

Recognition and development of women's human capacity is related directly to productivity. An African colleague, who is a manager of a national grain-marketing board, made this point recently when he remarked that incentives for production are significantly reduced by the common government policy of paying men for the sale of grain produced by women. The men receive the payment because they are designated legal heads of households or legal holders of the land, even though the women make the decision as to what and how much to produce. The men frequently spend the cash on goods or entertainment that do not benefit the family. If the women have no incentive to produce beyond subsistence, the entire economy loses because there is less grain to distribute in urban areas, or to export. The women and their families lose because rural families increasingly need cash for school fees, transport, inputs into farming activity, and goods that cannot be produced locally. And if rural women have no cash and no incentives to be economically productive, the cycle of rural poverty remains unbroken.[23]

Convention Article 14 states quite clearly that governments should acknowledge rural women's roles in development and ensure that they benefit from it. Acknowledging rural women's special problems and special knowledge, the article further requires their participation in development planning, education and training, credit and agricultural schemes, and community (public) life.[24] This article is unique as a statement of human rights because it emphasizes the rights of a particular sub-group to which special attention should be paid. Indeed, it reflects the tenor of the entire convention in emphasizing that human rights should not be assumed to be achieved until every group within society has demonstrably achieved them.

A key element of a just development policy is provision for women to own and manage property.[25] Both rural and urban women frequently are precluded by law or custom from owning, inheriting, and managing property and from access to credit. This is essentially a human rights issue and a question of justice. People who cannot own property are forever dependent. People who can be excluded from their homes and livelihoods on the whim of relatives (husbands or in-laws) are, by definition, lesser beings. Where women cannot borrow money without their husbands' or fathers' permission, or where they face greater burdens of proof as to ability to repay than men, their economic capacity is severely diminished. Property is fundamental to economic identity, and exclusion of an entire group of people from access to it, solely on the ground that they are women, is a denial of a basic element of their human identity.

Development programmes that do not take the property issue into account cannot produce sustainable results. A USAID programme evaluation has found that women are prevented from benefiting from a large proportion of development programmes because they do not have full legal status, including the right to own, use and manage property.[26] A human rights expert recently noted that aid evaluations for Danida and NORAD have produced similar conclusions.[27]

Under convention Articles 13, 14, 15, and 16, governments are obligated to change laws and policies to provide women with access to property and credit.[28] Because property relations are particularly tied to family relations, it is no accident that most of the property rights articulated in the convention are reiterated in Article 16. That article obligates governments to provide women with equal property rights during marriage and in divorce. Equal rights to inheritance are also implicit in Article 16.

The link between property rights and family relations is a key to the obstacles to convention implementation in every country. It is also a key to the possibilities.

Overcoming Obstacles to Implementation of Women's Human Rights: Custom and Tradition

The convention is a revolutionary document that couches its obligations in evolutionary language. Full implementation of women's human rights requires a fundamental change in the relationships between men and women, from subordination of women to full partnership between women and men. Successful partnership requires negotiation with respect between parties and a willingness to forego assumptions about roles and responsibilities.

The language and the legal requirements of the convention are evolutionary precisely because the premise is so dramatic. It is not contemplated that relationships between men and women, and between female citizens and their governments, will change overnight. But it is expected that governments will 'take all appropriate measures' to move forward on these issues.

In doing so, they must take on the issue of custom. From the fundamental right to freedom of association to the right to be free from violence directed specifically at women, women's human rights are consistently denied on the grounds that the violative laws or behaviour are 'customary' and are essential to the preservation of culture. In the name of custom, women are secluded from public view in a form of gender apartheid. They are beaten and even murdered by men and older women in their families if they behave in ways not prescribed by 'custom', and the abusers' behaviour is defended as 'custom'. They are precluded from inheriting property because 'custom' dictates that control of property accrues to men,[29] and they are left destitute as widows when male relatives, claiming customary prerogatives, force them from family property and fail to support the surviving family as 'custom' theoretically requires.[30] They are relegated to less remunerative jobs than men because 'custom' prevents them from being seen as the family breadwinner or from having authority over men in the workplace. The violations and contexts are varied; the defence of 'custom and culture' is universal.

CEDAW obligates governments to take on the issue of custom (Article 5). Few countries have reserved on this article. In ratifying the treaty, states agree to 'take all appropriate measures . . . to modify the social and cultural patterns of conduct of men and women, with a view to achieving the elimination of prejudices and customary and all other practices which are based on the idea of the inferiority or the superiority of either of the sexes or on stereotyped roles for men and women. . . .'

This issue cuts across all areas of the convention and must be addressed in all areas of state and NGO action. It is particularly difficult to address because custom is an expression of the culture in which people live, and frequently it is cited as the 'true' expression of who people are – tied closely to personal and community identity. Women's roles are a central element of this identity; the expression 'our women' or '[nationality/ethnic group] women' is commonly used, even by feminists, in discussions describing a culture or an ethnic group.[31] Protection of a particular immutable view of women is identified as protection of ethnic or national identity. Challenge and change are, from this perspective, seen as threats to custom and to identity.

Custom, as understood by many who cherish it most, is neither ossified nor fragile. It should be seen as a living expression of a culture's history and future. Defined as the way people live, as opposed to the way rigid traditionalists claim they used to live and should now live, custom constantly changes in response to changing conditions. Research indicates that communities continuously develop new customs, incorporating some old standards and discarding those that are no longer viable, to meet new conditions.[32]

This is not to say that state intervention may not be necessary to bring laws into parallel with changing customs,[33] or to establish equality standards that respond to contemporary circumstances but with which not all communities or community members may agree.[34] The international standards of the CEDAW and other human rights treaties are applicable in all ratifying countries regardless of custom and culture. The key element in the resolution of this issue is creativity – and sometimes courage – in bringing the international norms to life in the local context. Sometimes a single individual must take on the definition of new community standards when the state lags. In Botswana, Unity Dow challenged the nationality law that prohibited her children from having Botswana citizenship because her husband, their father, is not a citizen of Botswana. In holding that the law violated constitutional and international human rights standards, the trial court said, 'the time that women were treated as chattels or were there to obey the whims and wishes of males is long past.'[35]

The human rights approach to preservation of custom and culture is that it should be respected as a living expression of community norms but must not be allowed to be used as a rationale for denial of human rights. The international community characterizes individuals whose actions are restricted by repressive states because of their political views as 'prisoners of conscience'. The public and private activities of billions of women throughout the world are restricted solely because they are women. They are for all practical purposes prisoners of culture. CEDAW provides a means of opening the prison of culture, freeing women to live as fully respected human beings and thereby to participate fully in development.

Overcoming Obstacles to Convention Implementation: Resources

Development with justice requires a new approach to deployment of financial and information resources. Women cannot make effective claims to rights in development if they do not have adequate information on human rights and on development programmes and projects. They cannot participate effectively if they are not adequately educated for responsibility. They cannot develop economically without access to cash, credit or other forms of property. In short, internal and external development aid must be directed at helping them solve the problems of rights, culture and economic opportunity according to international standards.

Thousands of women's groups throughout the world have been organized with the ostensible purpose of improving women's situation. Too few of them include education about rights in their mission, or education on how to claim rights and deal with governments on these issues. Those that do must be supported if women are to become full partners in development.

Any impulse on the part of governments to change laws and processes to enhance women's rights in development should be encouraged. Governments should be reminded of their international obligations under the CEDAW and other treaties. Donors as well as recipient countries are bound by international human rights principles and should incorporate these principles in their development programmes if they are to succeed in the long term.

Programme approaches to meet the goal of development with justice include:

1. Human rights education programmes for women. With broader aims than legal literacy, programmes should include a component on civil and political rights and organizing to develop constituencies of women that can help create national and local political and cultural will for change.

2. Research on the living law and on the uses and misuses of custom and religion with respect to women's human rights. The successful method developed by the Women and Law in Southern Africa Research Project looks closely at how people actually live with the laws they have, to determine where changes should be made to make real improvements in women's lives. Such research should document current custom, as well as attitudes, degree of use of formal law, and experiences in courts and other tribunals. A global project along these lines, examining women's experience and status under Islamic law in 26 countries, is currently under way, coordinated by the Women Living Under Muslim Laws project.[36]

3. Projects to develop women's understanding of government and civil society. Citizen empowerment is at the heart of development with justice and is crucial to political stability and economic security.

4. National and international projects, including networks, that monitor international developments in women's human rights and help local and national groups use these developments at the national level. Much of this work is performed on a network basis rather than through formal organizations. The networks consist of organizations and individuals that provide information to each other, exchange experiences, and develop global or regional as well as national strategies to pursue women's human rights.

5. Rethinking and reforming education, from primary through university level, and including informal education and media projects, to address the fundamental problem of gender stereotyping that results in discrimination and denial of human rights.

Conclusion

Sustainable development will only be achieved when it is planned and programmed in the framework of delivering justice. Justice for women in the development context requires placing them at the starting point of planning. It requires providing the means for them to participate in the planning and benefit from the programmes as fully responsible adults. It means establishing their rights as human beings to make choices freely and responsibly, according to the standards of the CEDAW. Development with justice requires placing women's human rights at the centre of the development agenda.

NOTES

1 The Universal Declaration of Human Rights provides in Article 2 that 'everyone is entitled to all the rights and freedoms set forth in this Declaration, without distinction of any kind, such as . . . sex.' The International Covenant on Civil and Political Rights and the International Covenant on Economic, Cultural, and Social Rights (Article 2(2) and Article 3) restate the principle of non-discrimination on the basis of sex (Article 2(2) of each), and each states explicitly that 'States Parties to the present Covenant undertake to ensure the equal rights of men and women to the enjoyment of all . . . rights set forth in the present Covenant' (Article 3 of each).

2 As two Zambian researchers recently pointed out, women do not automatically benefit from a transition to democracy. A study of the 1991 Zambian elections found that women were not effectively encouraged to run for office, and neither national nor international human rights activists seemed to care whether women played a role in the electoral process. S. H. Longwe and Roy Clarke, *A Gender Perspective on the Zambian General Election of October 1991* (Zambia Association for Research and Development, December 1991) (available from IWRAW).

3 See CEDAW General Recommendation No. 19 (Twelfth Session, 1992). The convention covers private as well as public acts.

4 CEDAW has stated unequivocally that the right to liberty and personal security is contained within the women's convention. This right is particularly important as a basis of the right to freedom from gender-specific violence, which impedes women's exercise of their fundamental freedoms. See General Recommendation No. 19 (1992).

5 See, e.g., Sandra Coliver, 'United Nations Machineries on Women's Rights: How Might They Better Help Women Whose Rights Are Being Violated?' in *New Directions in Human Rights*, eds E. Lutz, H. Hannum and K. Burke (1989) University of Pennsylvania Press, Philadelphia; Andrew Byrnes, 'The "Other" Human Rights Treaty Body: The Work of the Committee on the Elimination of Discrimination Against Women', *Yale Journal of International Law* 14, 1–67 (1989); H. Charlesworth, C. Chinkin and S. Wright, 'Feminist Approaches to International Law', *American Journal of International Law* 85, 613–45 (1991).

6 The Committee in its reviews of country reports asks questions about facts and policies that are not included in the reports.

7 At its Eleventh Session, CEDAW considered the suggestion of the Expert Group Meeting on Violence Against Women (Vienna, 11–15 November 1991) that Optional Protocols to the convention be adopted concerning the subject of violence against women. Acknowledging the significance of the enforcement issue, the committee concluded that Optional Protocols on violence were an inappropriate remedy because they would 'undermine the importance of other topics of the convention . . . most members agreed that general comments made by the Committee on the articles of the convention would assist States Parties in implementing the convention by clarifying its scope' (Report of CEDAW, 1992, Eleventh Session, Section V: Ways and Means of Implementing Article 21 of the Convention).

8 This is the underlying reason for the large number of reservations (see R. Cook, 'Reservations to the Convention on the Elimination of All Forms of Discrimination Against Women', *Virginia Journal of International Law* 30, 643–716 (Spring 1990). Governments seem to see major long-term obstacles to compliance as to many issues, particularly in the areas of family law and nationality.

9 Unity Dow is a Botswana national married to an American. Their children were all born in Botswana and have lived there all their lives. Under Botswana law, children born to a married couple took the nationality of the father regardless of where the children were born. Dow's children therefore had no citizenship rights in their country of birth and she had no rights to pass on her nationality to them. In 1990 Dow challenged this law on the basis of

sex discrimination under the Botswana constitution and international law. The government took a very strong stand, claiming that Botswana culture is by nature discriminatory and the constitution should be interpreted accordingly. Dow won in the trial court in June 1991 and on appeal in July 1992. *Dow v. Attorney General*, MISCA 124/90 (High Court of Botswana, June 1991), affirmed, Appeal Court of Botswana, 3 July 1992.

10 Human Rights Watch Women's Rights Project, for example, has issued two studies focusing on abuses of women's human rights: *Criminal Injustice: Violence Against Women in Brazil* (1991), and *Double Jeopardy: Police Abuse of Women in Pakistan* (1992). Women Living Under Muslim Laws issues special alerts on abuses of women's human rights in the name of Islamic law as well as documents on developments in particular countries that affect women's freedoms (such as the June 1992 *Special Bulletin on Fundamentalism and Secularism in South Asia*). Amnesty International and Physicians for Human Rights also have projects on women's human rights, performed within the limits of their respective mandates. The Amnesty model of pressuring governments by citing particular cases and persecuted individuals, while useful in shedding light on the issues, is not appropriately designed to influence entire sociolegal systems and cultures.

11 Arvonne Fraser, 'Establishing Women's Human Rights', in *Women and Politics in the United Nations*, ed. Margaret Galey (forthcoming). This chapter includes an account of the drafting of the convention on the Elimination of All Forms of Discrimination Against Women and its precursor, the Declaration on the Elimination of Discrimination Against Women.

12 Women and Law in Southern Africa is a six-country (Botswana, Lesotho, Mozambique, Swaziland, Zambia and Zimbabwe; regional coordination in Harare) research project, started in 1988. It has undertaken an ambitious research programme to determine how women use the law, how the law treats women, and what should be done to change laws to improve women's lives. The project completed its first two-year research programme, on maintenance, in 1991 and is currently in the midst of its second two-year phase, focusing on inheritance law.

13 Women and Law in Southern Africa Research Project, *A Framework for Analysis of African Customary Law in Terms of the Women's Convention* (Harare, August 1992). Executive summary available from IWRAW.

14 Under the supremacy clause of the United States Constitution, for example, treaties may be considered the law of the land, but any treaty may be – and many are – ratified with a reservation that requires implementing legislation in order to make its principles effective. In many countries implementing legislation is required to make any treaty applicable in national law.

15 See Bangalore Principles, in *Developing Human Rights Jurisprudence, Vol. 1: Judicial Colloquium on the Domestic Application of International Human Rights Norms* (Commonwealth Secretariat, 1988). These principles were reaffirmed by groups of African jurists in two subsequent colloquia (Harare, 1989; Banjul, 1990). The decision in the Dow case, discussed above, is an example of using ratification of an international treaty to lend weight to constitutional interpretation.

16 In the last ten years, studies have been undertaken in over 30 states in the US to determine the level and extent of gender discrimination in the court system. See, e.g., *Report of the Minnesota Supreme Court Task Force for Gender Fairness in the Courts*, reprinted in *William Mitchell Law Review* 827 (1989); 'Report of the New York Task Force on Women in the Courts', *Fordham Urban Law Journal* 8 (1986–87).

17 A Ugandan writer made this point in a 1991 article in *Arise*, an activist Ugandan women's magazine. See *Women's Watch*, Vol. 5, No. 1 (July 1991). The issue is a universal one, as the gender task force studies (note 16) indicate.

18 Naina Kapur, speaking at the 1991 IWRAW International Workshop on Women's Human Rights and Reproductive Rights, described the horrendous court backlog in India that makes legal redress difficult even for the well-off.

19 Farida Shaheed, speaking at the 1990 IWRAW meeting, New York.

20 Fraser, *op. cit.*, describes the debate and the process of drafting these principles: developing countries insisted that the establishment of women's rights was critical to development, while industrialized countries took the position that the convention should address only social welfare issues.

21 The vote on the convention as a whole in the General Assembly was 130 – 0, with eleven abstentions (Bangladesh, Brazil, Comoros, Djibouti, Haiti, Mali, Mauritania, Mexico, Morocco, Saudi Arabi, Senegal). Fraser, *op. cit.*

22 In its eleventh session, CEDAW took note of the increasing number of female-headed households throughout the world, reflecting statistics and dialogues from the country report review process. CEDAW/C/1992.

23 Justin Mutasa, Zimbabwe, November 1991.

24 It is important to note that this article was offered by India during the drafting of the convention and was co-sponsored by five other developing countries as well as the GDR and the US. Fraser, *op. cit.*

25 While most development literature focuses on *land* as the most significant property interest – and in most rural communities it is – women also need access to the other forms of property, such as houses, buildings, businesses, livestock and farm equipment, household goods, cash – whatever people use and accumulate in their economic lives.

26 *Women in Development: A Report to Congress by the U.S. Agency for International Development FY89-FY90*, p. 65.

27 Katerina Tomaševski, informal communication, 1992.

28 In addition to access to property and credit, governments and NGOs should consider that education in the management of property and the establishment of businesses is important for women as few learn these skills at their fathers' knees.

29 Even in regions in which customary descent is matrilineal, the usual pattern is that descent is traced through the female line but males have control of the property.

30 Chuma Himonga, 'Property Disputes in Law and Practice: Dissolution of Marriage in Zambia,' in *Women and Law in Southern Africa*, eds A. Armstrong and W. Ncube (1987), Zimbabwe Publishing House, Harare.

31 For an illuminating discussion of this issue, see Thandabantu Nhlapo, 'The African Family and Women's Rights: Friends or Foes?,' *Acta Juridica* 1991, 135–46.

32 Recent research on the use of inheritance law in southern Africa has discovered that in some places the customary approach has changed, to allow women to inherit land. A. Armstrong, 'Internalising International Women's Rights Norms: What Do Women Really What?' paper presented to Workshop on Institutionalizing Human Rights in Southern Africa, University of Zimbabwe, 21–25 September 1992. In Mozambique, custom is continuously reshaped and redefined by the community courts, which resolve disputes according to the community standard rather than according to a stated body of customary law.

33 One of the most stunning examples of this is the dramatic change from fault-based to no-fault divorce law in many countries, as legislatures recognized that consensual marriage dissolution was becoming a norm.

34 Such as legal abolition of employment discrimination, affirmative action in education and employment, or the enactment of a uniform standard such as the Zimbabwe Legal Age of Majority Act (1982), which was written and has been interpreted to eliminate many sex-discriminatory aspects of customary practice.

35 *Dow* v. *Attorney General*, MISCA 124/90 (High Court of Botswana, June 1991), affirmed, Appeal Court of Botswana, 3 July 1992.

36 The need for this project has been stated by CEDAW. In its Sixth Session (1987), CEDAW requested that a study of Islam be prepared for use by the Committee in reviewing reports, in light of the volume of reservations and claims based on Islamic law. The request was roundly rejected by the General Assembly. The work therefore must be done by NGOs.

17

Aid Conditionality as a Lever for Women's Equality: Help or Hindrance?

ELIZABETH MCALLISTER[1]

Since the 1944 Bretton Woods conference, international lenders and aid agencies have used pre-set conditions attached to loans and aid to regulate the behaviour of the international economy. At first, conditionality was used to maximize the probability of loan repayment. With the introduction of stabilization and structural adjustment programmes by the International Monetary Fund (IMF) and World Bank, conditionality evolved to encompass requirements for borrowers to implement broad public policy reforms aimed at removing policy-induced obstacles to economic growth. For some time, aid conditionality has been used by some bilateral donors in pursuit of geopolitical and domestic interests, and by multilateral donors to ensure developmental effectiveness and financial responsibility.

Since the mid-1980s, there have been strong currents pushing for conditionality to extend to political reform too. The dramatic events in Eastern Europe and the former Soviet Union, along with the emergence of democratic regimes in Latin America and other parts of the world, have led to a growing public interest in and attention to issues of political development in the broadest sense – that is, human rights, democratization, and good governance.

There has also been a growing recognition among development planners that, for development to be effective and sustainable, it must promote political reform. In support of the post-Cold War trends in the developing world towards more open societies, and as a reflection of domestic public concern, the industrialized countries are putting more emphasis on the link between aid and human rights, good governance and democratization. Leaders of the OECD countries have signalled their intent to use the instruments of foreign policy, including conditions linked to Official Development Assistance (ODA), to favour reformers and to penalize non-reformers.

The new international agenda – globalization, democratization, demilitarization, and self-determination – has focused attention on aid conditionality. Experience to date has shown that it has been a positive influence in, for example, promoting improved monitoring of human rights violations. But conditionality can be controversial, complex and not without

106

costs to both recipients and donors.

Does it make sense to try to make multilateral and bilateral aid conditional on recipient countries meeting the standards of the Convention on the Elimination of All Forms of Discrimination Against Women (CEDAW) and the Forward-Looking Strategies (FLS)? That key question must be answered in the context of the experience with other forms of conditionality – both economic and political. Lessons can also be drawn from what we have learned in implementing existing donor policies on Women in Development.

The Complexity of Conditionality

THE IMPORTANCE OF COOPERATION

UNCED (the United Nations Conference on Environment and Development) has been described as a turning point in the North–South relationship, where the concept of donor and recipient countries gave way to an approach based on shared obligations and benefits. It is clear that many of the problems facing us – the economy, the environment, drug trafficking, arms proliferation, AIDS, terrorism, migration pressures – cannot be solved by countries within their own borders. Cooperation and mutual respect among countries are necessary preconditions for dialogue leading to integrated solutions that will benefit all parties.

When we refer to conditionality we are really talking about visible conditionality versus what used to be called quiet diplomacy. Visible conditionality is satisfying – you can report on it – and it does lend affirmation to groups fighting for human rights within a society by providing an international standard. The problem is that visible conditionality can be used not only to address goals achieved but also as a punishment.

Because conditionality is resented, it can jeopardize the cooperation required to address international issues. There are three sources of resentment against conditionality:

• it is regarded as an invasion of sovereignty;

• it almost always reflects power inequalities;

• it carries the implicit or explicit message that donors know better than recipients what is good for them and what their priorities should be.

Even if traditional notions of sovereignty are being eroded year after year by the growing consensus about the new international agenda, there is still plenty of scope based on the other two counts: inequality and donor arrogance.[2]

The need for international cooperation and the risks posed by using conditionality are best exemplified in the area of the environment. The trade-off between concerns to protect the global environment and a desire to defend human rights poses a dilemma for donors: the countries whose support is most needed on environmental issues are often those with poor or mixed human rights records. If donors enter into an adversarial relationship with a large country having a poor human rights record, it can be difficult to maintain a relationship that supports cooperation in advancing global environmental programmes.

DEVELOPMENT ASSISTANCE AS LEVERAGE

Development assistance can mean access to new ideas. It can provide resources and encouragement to women's and other human rights groups. Cutting off aid could be precisely the wrong thing to do if it eliminates the continued presence of aid-sponsored individuals who contribute new ideas. It is the impact of new ideas on the local people involved in development cooperation that gives donors real leverage, and offers the best chance of long-term change in attitudes and behaviour. Pre-Tiananmen, Canada sponsored over 300 young Chinese post-graduate students a year. Now, we receive fewer, older individuals for under one year. We have lost a potent lever: showing a critical mass of potential leaders, men and women, what it is like to live in a free and open society – one that is relatively active in promoting equity for women.

By cutting off aid, we can be playing into the hands of the repressive elements of a society who like nothing better than to see donors go home, taking their perceived subversive human rights ideals with them. In leaving a country, we throw away opportunities to influence the policy agenda in many direct and indirect ways.

Specific conditionality can also play into the hands of hardliners who can use our requirements to accuse the reformers of being puppets of the West. Otherwise put, we risk discrediting desirable reforms by making them seem externally imposed. For example, African women have made the case that Western support for eliminating female circumcision undermines their efforts by forcing them to deal with accusations of foreign influence by Western feminists.

BILATERAL VS MULTILATERAL LEVERAGE

Conditionality – whether imposed multilaterally or bilaterally – will have little impact on countries that are not dependent on aid. In numerous other cases where a country is aid dependent, any one bilateral donor's aid may amount to just a fraction of the partner country's development budget. Cutting ODA in these situations involves virtually no incentive for the government to change. The only effective way for a bilateral donor to take punitive measures is through the coordinated pressure of many donors. Kenya is a recent case in point: the refusal of donors to pledge at the 1991 consultative group appeared to prompt the Kenyan president to reconsider his resistance to democratic change, and may potentially help to bring about a multi-party system.

Coordination is not always easy. Donors' policies may differ as to what constitutes a case deserving a major intervention, and the country in question may be of greater importance to one donor than to others, for historical or strategic reasons. Achieving donor consensus on conditionality regarding women's rights is sure to face more headwinds than any other category of human rights.

CONFLICT WITH OTHER FOREIGN POLICY OBJECTIVES

Any bilateral donor's foreign policy relationship with a partner country is a complex web of interests, including trade, commerce, environmental protection, peace and security. For example, Canada's prosperity depends on trade, and the aid programme helps to establish long-term trade linkages with developing countries which provide immediate benefits to Canadian firms. Our trade interests have not prevented Canada from taking a leadership role in the human rights arena, but those interests are inevitably a factor in the decision-making process that precedes a decision to impose conditionality. In all countries, balancing the conflicting demands between, and even among, similar domestic interest groups is a challenge. The promotion of human rights must be firmly based on a realistic analysis of what can be achieved, and what is compromised in the process, including the human rights objective itself.

COMPROMISING THE VICTIM

A key consideration in cutting or reducing aid because of human rights abuses is the problem of a double penalty – victims suffer abuse from their governments, and then lose access to the resources and support provided by aid. By cutting Canadian aid to any developing country where we have a strong bilateral programme on the basis of a contravention of civil and political rights, we would lose ground on the gains we have made in our active, country-specific WID strategies. If we cut our aid, and thus our programmes, many women would lose their lifeline to like-minded women in other developing countries and in Canada. There is also the question of how we calibrate conditionality when a recipient makes progress in one area of human rights but falters in another.

COSTS TO THE DONOR

Aid is expensive to turn off. Costs are high in terms of lost investment in planning and preparation. Contracts must be cut, trainees and cooperants returned home mid-programme. Relationships that have taken years to build are lost and the ability to dialogue is soured. As argued by Joan Nelson of the Overseas Development Council:

Conditionality can deflect dialogue between the partners from substance to procedure and bargaining. Moreover, designing and monitoring and enforcing conditions can consume a great deal of donor time and resources that might perhaps be better put towards other tasks, including developing a deepened grasp of [the issues], broader contacts within the developing country, and more imaginative design of projects to support improved governance and democratic reform.[3]

CONCLUSION

Conditionality presents an array of subtleties, complications, contradictions and understandings. The complexity has only been covered partially above. For example, the difficulty of defining what is a universal right, and what is a Western concept of a human right, has sparked a major debate in itself – one of particular relevance to those of us trying to improve the status of women on the global front.

Clearly, conditionality is not a strategy in itself in achieving reform, but it can complement broader intervention strategies. Its use has to be carefully weighed against the risks and the costs to recipient and donor, and especially to the people it is meant to support.

A decision to mount an effort to require donors to use conditionality to advance women's rights must be weighed carefully in comparison with other strategies. It is discouraging to see how seldom women's rights are even mentioned in the literature or in the debates on human rights and conditionality. It is tempting therefore to argue that bilateral and multilateral assistance must from now on be conditional on countries meeting the standards of the CEDAW and the Forward Looking Strategies. But valuable time and effort could be lost in what could be fruitless efforts to secure multiple donor support. On the more positive side, the debate would at least focus attention on women's rights.

If such an effort *were* successful, implementation would be hampered by the fact that the Convention and the FLS are broad programmatic statements that call for extensive institutional and societal change over the long term to realize their intent. For example, how would donors measure or enforce compliance with CEDAW's Article 5, which requires nation states 'to take all appropriate measures to modify the social and cultural patterns of conduct of men and women, with a view to achieving the elimination of prejudices. . .'?

Experience of compliance with economic conditionality indicates that compliance tends to be high for single-shot measures required of a few central officials, in contrast to reforms that depend on an extended series of decisions and actions and the cooperation of multiple agencies.[4] It is likely, therefore, that conditionality could be more effective in instances where donors would require the repeal of a sexist law or the release of imprisoned women activists.

The question thus raised is: how do we ensure that, when conditionality is used for advancing human rights, women's rights are included?

Lessons Learned from CIDA's Women in Development Strategies

MOVE FROM ADVOCACY TO ACCOUNTABILITY

Women's groups were exasperated with donors who had sent mission after mission to Namibia to work on the establishment of the Constituent Assembly but who only at the last minute did a desk-top analysis of the implications for Namibian women. In Namibia, as in many other countries that have survived strife to make the transition to democratic rule, women-headed families often predominate. The omission of women's participation was not so much a question of the lack of conditionality in support of women's rights and participation, as a symptom of the failure of the donor agencies to hold staff accountable for gender issues.

The strength of the Canadian International Development Agency's Women in Development strategy lies in its success in defining the question as an economic and developmental issue as well as a matter of equity. It professionalizes WID by moving gender issues from being a matter of personal persuasion to one of professional responsibility. In the 1980s, CIDA replaced its internal advocacy approach with an accountability and feedback system built into the existing organizational structure. The President's Committee defined the policy and organizational objectives – the 'what', top down – and a cross-organizational committee with broad membership built the 'how' from the bottom up. In this process of consensual negotiation, ownership for WID was moved out of a small WID Directorate into the mainstream and into the mandates of all programmes and services.

I would suggest that rather than trying to convince donors to apply conditionality (on meeting the standards of the CEDAW and the FLS) to recipient countries, and rather than striving to find reasonable ways of enforcing such conditionality, efforts could be more effectively aimed at ensuring that WID accountability is *built into the internal reward systems* of multilateral and other aid agencies. If WID accountability is defined, then women's issues will finally be included in broader political conditionality when it is used, and more resources will be applied to the kinds of programmes outlined in the FLS.

An excellent start has been made in moving donors towards accepting a systemic, accountability approach to WID. The OECD Development Assistance Committee (DAC) Experts' Group on Women in Development was successful in strengthening the accountability approach in the 'Revised Guiding Principles on Women in Development, 1989'. Donors are not compelled to implement the Guiding Principles, but their approval by the DAC donors has been used successfully by interest groups to push for the adoption of strengthened WID policies by their national aid agency.

NEGOTIATING PROACTIVE PROGRAMMES AND PROJECTS

Once donors have made a commitment to WID, a number of channels are available for achieving the goals of the CEDAW and the FLS. In my experience, the key is the ability to negotiate gender-based strategies, programmes and projects with the partner country. As renowned negotiator Roger Fisher outlines, negotiating depends on the power of:

- skill and knowledge;
- a good relationship – including trust and an ability to communicate easily and effectively;
- an elegant solution;
- legitimacy;
- commitment;
- a good alternative to negotiating, in this case conditionality.

To cite an example, during negotiations with regard to a $26 million oil and gas project in China, CIDA asked that 20 per cent of the trainees should be women and that 20 per cent of management positions should be filled by women. The Chinese insisted that we guarantee the same ratio for the Canadian executing agency. The tougher negotiation was in the oil patch in Canada! This shows that even when projects have a commercial aspect, there is scope to bring women into non-traditional occupations – in Canada as well as in other countries.

Rather than taking an adversarial stance, we need to try to build a collaborative relationship with men in promoting and supporting the rights of women, whether it is within CIDA or within developing countries. The men save face; they can come on board and move with us to where we're wanting to go.

Sometimes it is hard to follow a collaborative approach, for example, when domestic violence is involved, but anger and emotion are not constructive. We need to build in the technical skills to measure discrimination and we need to appoint women (and men) to work on women's issues who have the technical expertise, the education, and an understanding of the law. We need positive proactive policy dialogue in efforts to empower women, and we must try to understand the story-behind-the-story in every country.

POLICY DIALOGUE

Policy dialogue is a major channel for negotiating WID interventions. As with our efforts to promote broader political reform, there have been very direct, substantive and productive discussions at consultative group meetings of bilateral donors and other donors. During our annual consultations with partner countries, Canada's policy on WID is raised as an issue of importance. Over time, and through the development of good working relationships, we have been able to help countries develop their own institutional arrangements for improving the status of women. We have secured their support for including gender analysis in the substance of projects and for building targets for women's participation into most of our bilateral projects (a kind of contractual conditionality, but it 'feels' more like a negotiated agreement among partners).

NATIONAL MACHINERIES

We have invested considerable resources in supporting national machineries in a number of countries. For example, the Women's Support Project in Indonesia works with the Ministry of State for the Role of Women. In preparation for Indonesia's next Five-Year Development Plan, the Ministry, with CIDA assistance, began a series of initiatives to 'engender the development planning process'. These involve: improving data gathering on the situation of women in Indonesia; developing gender analysis training modules for use in all government training programmes for civil servants; initiating a system to monitor the participation of women in all development training plans; enhancing the capacity of researchers in women's study centres; and providing skill training for Ministry staff.

NON-GOVERNMENTAL ORGANIZATIONS

We have supported non-governmental women's organizations in their efforts to have women's rights respected. In Kenya, for instance, the Small Projects Fund for women helps women's groups translate civic material into local languages in order to create awareness about their existing rights. In Zimbabwe, the University of Ottawa Law Foundation is educating paralegals to disseminate information on rights to women. In Asia, we provide support to the Asia–Pacific Forum on Women, Law and Development which is working to promote greater respect for women's rights.

MULTILATERAL ORGANIZATIONS

Canada has been active in promoting women's rights and women's issues at the governing councils of international aid organizations. For example, in 1989 CIDA seconded a staff member as senior co-ordinator to UNHCR to assist in ensuring that refugee women could participate in and benefit equitably from all aspects of UNHCR programmes. She has been successful in seeing policy and guidelines for the protection of women refugees approved by UNHCR's executive committee. Because of her work, the country delegations have agreed to convert her position to a permanent one in the UNHCR executive branch. Thus, for a minimum investment, we have been able to realize a significant return in policy and programme change for refugee women.

As issues become more globalized, the UN system becomes increasingly important. In a wide variety of situations like the UNHCR, Canada has been able to increase its leverage on women's issues beyond the size of our contribution. This is another way donors can ensure that actions for improving women's status are set in motion.

Conclusion

Conditionality is effective only when:

• conditions are well-defined and closely monitored;

• the benefits of compliance are clearly greater for the recipient country than the costs;

• economic and political costs on the donor are less than the benefits sought through conditionality.

This is a tall order by any measure.

The complexity of conditionality in general, as well as the programmatic and long-term focus of the CEDAW and the FLS in particular, argue against efforts to make bilateral and multilateral assistance conditional on recipient countries meeting the standards of the CEDAW and implementing the FLS. Strategies to incorporate accountability for WID into the internal organizational reward systems of donor agencies will be more productive in ensuring that women's rights are included in human rights conditionality, and that specific abuses of women's rights will be raised when necessary. Implementation by bilateral donors of the OECD-DAC Guiding Principles on Women in Development will result in greater participation by women in the design, management and rewards of development programmes, while improving the developmental impact of ODA.

Experience tells us that partnership and negotiation with developing countries is the most effective way to realize the goals of the Convention. Assistance to women's organizations in developing countries, aimed at empowering their voices and strengthening their ability to influence national priorities, is a necessary accompanying strategy.

Notes

1   The author wishes to express her appreciation to Ann Brazeau of the UNHCR and to Linda Ervin, Dr Soe Lin, and Allan Thornley, CIDA colleagues, for their insights and inspiration.

2   J. Nelson and S. Eglinton, 'Encouraging Democracy: What Role For Conditioned Aid?' Overseas Development Council, Policy Paper No. 4 (April 1992), p. 18.

3   *Ibid.*, p. 44.

4   *Ibid.*, p. 31.

18

The UN, World Conferences and Women's Rights

BARBARA ADAMS

The United Nations is, on the one hand, a place where statements of ideals are articulated and standards of conduct set, particularly in the area of human rights. On the other hand, the UN is a place which reflects the inequalities of the power distribution within and among member states; it is a place where decision making is not as independent of national government priorities as its image would suggest.

On the one hand, the UN is a place where there is democracy in terms of the issues on its agenda. Issues, like apartheid, that could not always be sustained on national or bilateral agendas, remain on the multilateral UN agenda. On the other hand, the UN is a place of elites.

The UN is an arena in which women have raised concerns and influenced agendas, particularly during the UN Decade for Women, through the CEDAW and with the monitoring of the Forward Looking Strategies. Yet, it is a male-dominated system, and this influences processes of decision making and concepts of participation. These influences are exacerbated by a hierarchical attitude towards international work rather than a horizontal approach which views international institutions as pieces which interlock with many others to make up a global puzzle.

The United Nations

The UN includes many work programmes and several approaches to that work. It is a donor, an organization for service, research, and information dissemination, and a place for advocacy. The work of some agencies, such as UNICEF's priority of the girl child, promote programme approaches that bring together women's rights and development concerns.

The United Nations conjures up many different images: the Secretary-General; peace-keeping forces; the Security Council; refugee work; UNICEF; the struggle against apartheid. Its agenda is comprehensive. It has many different agencies and programmes. These come together in the agenda of the General Assembly.

The General Assembly, the highest political body of the UN, is made up of all 179 member states. The permanent representatives of governments to the UN General Assembly come from foreign ministries, and they come to promote and protect the foreign policy of their governments. Consequently, the UN today is free from the Cold War stalemate and continues to reflect both changes in the international agenda and the prevailing status quo.

Today, the UN is very involved in trying to resolve regional conflicts, in peacekeeping and in humanitarian assistance. This focus is having an impact on the decision-making processes in the UN, with the Security Council taking the lead and emphasizing the power and influence of its permanent members. In practice, this means decision making is moving into the domain of a small circle of players. Aside from the impact on the issues, this approach is less participatory, less friendly and more inaccessible to women.

Over the last few decades, the UN system has evolved into a disparate structure with little coordination and some duplication. These weaknesses and the concept of a 'unitary UN' have become the focus of attention of the Secretary-General and some member states, especially the major contributors to the UN budget. The concept of UN consolidation involves improving the division of responsibilities among programmes and specialized agencies. A number of member states, especially developing countries, have expressed concern at the impact of this rationalization on the economic agenda of the UN. They fear that macroeconomic policies will be the sole preserve of the World Bank, the IMF and the GATT, agencies whose policies they believe are dominated by the major industrialized countries.

Another consequence of the changes underway at the UN is the increased openness to outside perspectives and outside expertise. This is complemented by an increase of attention to the practice of governance, as part of the emphasis on 'democratization'. All this creates greater space for NGO participation. This latter development is evident in the procedures adopted for the UN Conference on Environment and Development and, more recently, for the International Conference on Population and Development. The rules of procedure for NGO participation in the UN Commission on Sustainable Development will indicate whether procedures for broader NGO participation in world conferences will be extended to the ongoing work of the UN.

The attention and enthusiasm given by member states to addressing governance is not extended to the question of resources. UN resources from member states have not increased while the work of the UN – particularly in the area of peacekeeping – has. The tightening of access to resources and the shift in resource distribution within the UN system is something that may have negative consequences for women's issues.

The year 1995 is a very important one for the UN, not because the fourth World Conference for Women will take place that year in Beijing, China (although it would be nice to say that is the reason). 1995 will mark the 50th anniversary of the UN and the culmination of efforts to reform and restructure the UN system in tune with global priorities. Concern has been expressed, whimsically but wisely, that while women will be meeting in Beijing, men will be in New York determining the world's priorities and the use of its resources.

World Conferences

Upcoming UN world conference themes cover human rights, population and development, social issues and women. The World Conference for Human Rights provides an opportunity to advance women's rights. In this context, there are other possibilities that should be examined: the International Conference on Population and Development in Cairo, the 1995 Social Summit hosted by Denmark, and the fourth World Conference for Women in Beijing.

Influencing national government positions is an important prerequisite to influencing a world conference. The decision, the negotiations and the outcomes of a world conference are based on negotiations between governments, in the context of foreign policy objectives. Involvement during the preparatory committee phase is essential since most of the negotiating work is completed before the conference begins, with only a few key issues left unresolved.

Prior to the Earth Summit in Rio de Janeiro, NGOs tended to concentrate their participation during world conferences on NGO parallel events rather than interacting with the official process. Traditional reasons for this tendency vary: some NGOs regarded international networking amongst NGOs as more relevant than the official process; some were unable to gain access to the official conference; some, upon realizing that the bulk of the negotiations had already been completed, look beyond the UN system.

It is important to distinguish between the international governmental mechanisms (such as the UN General Assembly or the World Conference for Human Rights) and the UN Secretariat in order to determine how and where decisions are made, and how NGOs can take part in these decisions. The UN Secretariat is the international civil service and the major administrative organ of the UN. It is headed by the Secretary-General who is appointed for a five-year term.

Establishing contact with a secretariat set up to service a conference is another way to access and influence the process. The secretariat is responsible for preparing background papers which are sometimes undertaken by consultants. Secretariats have tended to be more comfortable with academics who publish in journals than with NGOs who work at the grassroots level.

NGO Approaches to World Conferences

Approaching a conference comprehensively by paying attention to all the agenda items is useful. NGOs often have expertise in specialized areas and consequently may find themselves unknowingly competing with other NGOs that are promoting different but not necessarily conflicting concerns and priorities. While this situation can reflect some of the competitiveness existing among NGOs, often it merely reveals a lack of both communication and networking.

Another reason for following the bigger picture is that negotiations go through a number of rounds or stages as governmental positions are prepared. The process can be likened to that of playing chess or of collective bargaining. A conference is a chessboard in which the various groupings of countries involved have certain priorities and work to position themselves to have the best negotiating hand when it comes to the last round.

Often NGOs attend a world conference with the objective of influencing the outcome. They come away having formed contacts and set up new and unexpected programmes. Establishing working contacts with NGOs that monitor the UN on a regular basis can be useful, especially in gathering information.

NGOs have been most effective in influencing the UN in the area of human rights. They have learned to use the system well. However, they seem to lack a collective institutional memory. Moreover, although a lot of knowledge has been gained, and a fair amount of experience exists, it is concentrated into a specialized area. Consequently there is little written information available for organizations coming for the first time to this type of UN work.

NGOs can face a dilemma when becoming more involved in inter-national networking and lobbying if these activities pull them away from their local or national work. This can lessen or undermine accountability to membership and to local communities. Often NGOs committed to grass-roots development work have a greater understanding of the root causes of problems, but do not or cannot follow the international agenda, which then does not benefit from their experiences and insights. At this time of increasing openness for NGOs at the UN, serious consideration should be given to the value of UN work as a NGO priority.

The next two years, with UN restructuring and refocusing, will be a key time to address and improve the procedures and the methods for ongoing consultation – a topic which may seem boring and tedious, but which can lay a firmer foundation for the participation of women and other voices of civil society in the coming decades.

19

Integrating, Not Separating, Women in Development

CAROLYN HANNAN-ANDERSSON

The move towards a new vision of human rights represents a special challenge for development cooperation – carried out through bilateral and multilateral agencies as well as non-governmental organizations. Firstly, on the policy level, the broadening of the predominant vision will require a change in attitudes and approaches; and secondly, at the level of practice, it will require development of methodologies and instruments for implementing new strategies.

This paper concentrates on the roles and responsibilities of bilateral donors, and on the most appropriate strategy for working effectively with women's rights as human rights within the context of development cooperation programmes. Already bilateral donors are doing a lot to incorporate a gender perspective into existing programmes which deal with social and economic rights, as well as to promote women's rights through support to networks and individual institutions/groups at all levels – usually through special funds. Less has been done in terms of incorporating a gender perspective in the increasing support to civil and political rights in many agencies.

The greatest challenge for bilateral donors is finding the most appropriate and effective means of incorporating the perspective of women's rights as human rights into the existing support to both civil and political rights and socio-economic development programmes. Support to special efforts to promote women's rights is less problematic, although there is a need to ensure that it is based on local priorities and needs and works towards long-term structural change in transforming women's rights. This will not simply require an increase in the number of separate inputs directed specifically to women, but rather a transformation of the whole mainstream agenda through the incorporation of a gender perspective.

However, it needs to be kept in mind that 'bilateral donors' are a very diverse group of agencies with varying mandates and resources. Some donors have gone further than others with efforts in the three areas mentioned above. In all agencies, there is an ongoing 'struggle' to ensure that a gender perspective is included in all support.

Learning from the Past: WID/Gender Experiences in Development Cooperation

Within development cooperation, a major problem has been the continued marginalization of the issue of women in development through its perception simply as a 'women's issue' – something outside the realm of the 'mainstream agenda', something to be taken care of by women. In practical terms, this has meant the relegation of responsibility for women in development to under-resourced units or desks staffed entirely by women. The issue of roles and responsibilities within organizations is a major one to be addressed if efforts to improve the situation of women are to encompass all areas of development cooperation.

It has also become increasingly clear that the role of special units working with women in development cooperation agencies should be catalytic, developing the awareness, commitment and capacity of those responsible for different programmes in all areas – health, forestry, infrastructure, agriculture – to ensure that everyone working in development cooperation is able to incorporate a gender perspective into their work. This means that focal points should not have an 'ownership complex' about the issues they are working with, but should work actively to ensure all personnel and consultants working with development cooperation can take on the issues as relevant in their particular work.

The problem of the negligence and abuse of women's rights being seen simply as a 'women's issue' is already clear. There is practical evidence that issues such as sexual harassment and abuse, rape, sexual abuse of children and wife battery are seen as women's issues (Ashworth, 1992), despite the fact that men are clearly involved – in the neglect and abuse of women's rights and in their predominance in the institutions which exist to ensure civil, political and socio-economic rights. To envision and work with women's rights as human rights successfully, it will be important to identify the roles and responsibilities of individuals and institutions. It will be necessary to sensitize and awaken commitment in both women and men.

Ashworth (1992) also points out that diplomats and 'experts' are surprisingly ignorant of the existing mechanism for securing and protecting women's rights, the Women's Convention of 1979, and that there is a trend 'to refer any issue relating to women or gender to a junior female colleague, instead of taking responsibility for it themselves.' The goal must be for all those working with human rights and development to see the gender implications and have the capacity to work with them. The onus is on women's groups/organizations/units working to promote women's rights to see that this transfer of responsibilities takes place.

In the human rights context the WID 'efficiency' rationale is being used more frequently. It has, for example, been promoted by UNIFEM in the sense of the negative developmental impact of the economic costs related to violence against women – for example costs related to court-time, policing, hospital/health-care costs, prisons and detention, and loss of productivity. It has also been pointed out that there are currently no indicators of human development, democracy or human freedom which take into account the unbalanced capacity of women and men to exercise and control resources. This has deep significance for effective and participatory development, genuine democracy and freedom (Ashworth, 1992). The statutory and customary barriers to women holding or inheriting property are also said not only to increase the impoverishment of women but to also hold back national development (Ashworth, 1992).

However, the efficiency approach can have a negative side which should be kept in mind. For example, the use of the rationale of reducing population size for promoting inputs in the area of family planning (under the guise of reproductive rights), as well as for promoting increased access to education and employment of women, undermines the human rights aspects and is thus detrimental to women.

Far too often women are still described simply as passive victims and categorized with children, minorities and the handicapped. This focus on women as a vulnerable group has done women a disservice. Instead of being seen as actors (often the major actors) and the crucial stakeholder in development, women are portrayed as conservative and passive, and the important roles they play remain invisible to planners.

Although 'welfare' principles in policy approaches to women in development have decreased in importance over recent years, there is an apparent re-emergence of these in the area of economic development. Women's economic roles/needs/rights are relegated to the 'welfare sphere'.

Similarly, in the area of environment, women's roles/needs/rights are often not given sufficient attention in planning and implementation.

There is already evidence of a 'vulnerable groups' approach within the area of human rights. For example, the very fact that social and economic rights 'were reduced to "basic needs" in development, leaving them to the compassion rather than the duty of states and the international community' (Ashworth, 1992), means that it is difficult to lift efforts in the area of socio-economic rights, particularly those of women, above the level of a welfare approach.

Ashworth (1992) also points to the trend to reduce the incidence of violence against women to 'a matter of victims rather than of criminal behaviour'. It facilitates the envisioning of women's rights as something separate, best dealt with by special, separate inputs through women's organizations. There is a need to beware of the same trend within the programmes of support being developed by donors and directed towards first generation human rights – civil and political rights. There is a real risk that donors will develop separate programmes of inputs for women with a focus on women as a vulnerable group.

There is an added risk, when separate funds are established for women's rights, that these funds will be used to support everything related to women. Separate funds can play an important role in consciousness-raising and empowerment, but there should be very clear objectives and criteria. Otherwise activities may develop in a very *ad hoc* manner. Given the existing difficulties with linkages between civil and political rights and socio-economic rights, the result could be difficulty in making any clear linkages between women's rights and human rights.

All bilateral donors (as well as multilateral and NGOs) can today point to concrete separate projects/inputs for women. While these have, of course, often been very positive, a major problem has been the fact that the 'mainstream agenda' has remained largely untouched. There is little evidence of a conscious policy or strategy to adapt the programmes as a whole to give adequate consideration to women's roles/needs/rights.

Agencies pushing for integration have targeted the incorporation of women's/gender aspects into all mainstream programmes. At times this has been an 'add women and stir' type of integrative approach. Such an approach has been opposed by many as it accepts the basic agenda as it is – with all the elements of mal(e) development. However, many donors utilizing an integrative approach have had a hidden agenda or unstated objective, i.e., through the experience gained in involving women as well as men in projects/programmes/inputs, to open the way for changes in policy and strategy, or, in other words, a transformation of the mainstream agenda in terms of both policy and practice.

In the area of human rights, the need for a transformative approach is clear. The strategy for achieving the transformation is less clear, especially since this requires that 'barriers be broken down between public and private, state and non-governmental responsibilities' (Bunch, 1992).

It is also clear that the concept of human rights is unacceptable because it is based on male norms and does not take into consideration the needs and rights of women. The 'add women and stir' concept of integration will not be adequate – there is a need for the transformation to impact on policy and practice in the mainstream, and for changes in attitudes within agencies to accommodate this shift of focus. Even those agencies which have a strong equity focus and a strong focus on human rights have not always recognized or emphasized women's rights in an integrated manner.

A WID equity approach is usually found in organizations with a strong overall equity approach – those which focus on promoting democratic development, economic independence, and social and economic equity. However, practical integration of the two policies – general equity and WID equity – is necessary if women's rights are to be treated as human rights. This integration is not automatic.

The lack of desegregation in terms of gender at household and community levels has been a hindrance to the development of adequate analysis methodologies and thus to the acquisition of adequate knowledge bases for planning.

The concept of gender – the social relationships between men and women arising from the particular division of roles, responsibilities, access to and control over resources and decision-making authority and needs/interests – has proven to be very useful in development cooperation contexts. In particular, the development of 'gender planning methodology', which attempts to apply the concept to specific planning contexts, has been useful. Where the methodology has been integrated into existing planning procedures, rather than through development of separate routines, it has been possible to identify the implications for adequate planning and thus to incorporate a gender perspective successfully in different types of support programmes.

In the human rights context, a similar lack of desegregation means that neglect and abuse of women's rights are not visible and thus not taken into account. The move to a transformation of the human rights concept requires a gender perspective.

As Eisler (quoted in Bunch, 1992) points out, an adequate approach to securing women's rights as human rights will require a refinement of the definition and measurement of human rights, since the yardstick developed has been based on the male as the norm. Working adequately with women's rights will require an understanding of the social relationships between women and men, and a re-examination of the patriarchal biases.

The role of donors in development cooperation is a supportive one. Donors should not 'own' the development cooperation programmes they support, but rather see their role as facilitating the development goals of the partner country. Real dialogue with partner countries is the basis of successful development cooperation programmes. Dialogue at different levels – national, regional, and district levels – with counterpart ministries and institutions is not adequate in itself. Such dialogue needs to be complemented by consultation with both women and men at different levels, down to the grassroots. This is essential if the programmes are to be based on felt needs and if real participation in the process is to be achieved. Too often programmes are inadequate, both in terms of dialogue and consultation, and this makes incorporation of a gender perspective difficult.

An important link can be made here to the policy approach referred to as 'empowerment'. The term 'empowerment' has been utilized in so many different contexts and in so many different ways that the real meaning or 'content' of the concept has become somewhat elusive. It is necessary to be aware of what 'empowerment' should imply. Empowerment does not mean developing the capacity of women to carry out agendas set for them from outside. Empowerment entails actual agenda setting and therefore requires consciousness-raising and development of capacity.

In the process of linking women's rights to human rights, dialogue will be an important tool. It will be important to establish open communication channels if donors are to try to pressure for ratification and adherence to the principles of the CEDAW, and include an adequate gender perspective in all inputs related to human rights.

The development of consultation is also important – for gaining knowledge and ensuring that all inputs are based on local priorities. Much of the backlash experienced after the initial equity approach in the 1970s was due to the fact that the approach was top-down and initiated from 'outside'. This was true, for example, of attempts to influence legislation. Experience showed that even if legislation was improved, little was achieved if women themselves did not know what their rights were or what they could do if their rights were violated. The grassroots dimensions became more apparent and this led to the development of legal literacy programmes in many countries, and to awareness of the need for more research into what women's needs/priorities are and how they are affected by legal instruments. For effective work in linking women's rights to human rights, it will be necessary for donors to understand the local needs, priorities, initiatives and resources. This will require considerable development of networks and knowledge bases.

Too often women and development efforts have been focused on treating the symptoms of women's problems rather than dealing with the causes. A typical example is in the area of health. If analysis is made of the causes of women's health problems, it becomes very clear that many are embedded in unequal gender relations – in terms of labour (workloads), responsibilities for family welfare, and access to resources and decision making. It is impossible to deal with women's health problems with the traditional focus on women alone. There must be a change in men's attitudes and actions if there is to be potential for long-term change in terms of women's health.

There is a need for more methodology development in analysis of problems. A positive development is the increasing move away from a sectoral 'project focus' to a more interdisciplinary approach which may lead to holistic analysis of problems, and identification of causes/constraints and potential for dealing with these.

There is a tendency towards the same approach in women's rights. Even here a more holistic approach should be advocated to put the specific problem tackled in a wider context. Then cause and effect can be seen more clearly and appropriate actions developed – whether through legal action or inputs in socio-economic development programmes.

For example, women's rights to become members of existing co-operatives and to equal access to existing credit schemes should be given more attention. Donors should concentrate more on identifying the constraints to women's involvement in cooperatives and finding means of overcoming these, than on establishing separate cooperatives and credit schemes for women. In terms of women's economic rights, more could be done to develop a gender perspective for incorporation into the main programmes, instead of concentrating all attention on compensatory 'social' programmes. More attention should be given to the informal sector, to women in administration and the civil service, and to the agricultural sector. The issue of land rights is also crucial for women. Most discussions of this problem do not have a gender perspective – even in countries moving towards a market system where radical changes are taking place with regard to access to land. Donors working in these countries should pay more attention to adequating gender analysis and identification of constraints to access, and to developing means for ensuring equal access.

Organizational Development and Strategy: Practical Implications for Development Cooperation Agencies

Given the lessons learned through past experience with involving women in development cooperation programmes, the following preconditions for effective work with women's rights as human rights in the context of the total development cooperation programmes can be determined.

The main requirement is an understanding of the expanded concept – women's rights as human rights – and a clear understanding of the practical implications for development cooperation. That is, that the expanded vision takes us beyond civil and political rights, makes necessary linkages with socio-economic and socio-cultural rights, and requires attention to the particular issue of violence against women.

The objective should be to incorporate a gender perspective into the analysis and planning processes which emphasizes women's rights as human rights in all areas of development cooperation, rather than simply increasing the number of separate programmes for women. Separate inputs for women in the area of human rights are necessary but they must be the result of a thorough gender analysis, and should be seen as complementary to the integrative approach.

A key input in a successful strategy must be the identification of the roles and responsibilities of all actors in the development cooperation agency. All personnel within the organization and all consultants should be aware of the relevance of the issue of women's rights as human rights for their work, and what concretely they can do in the context of their normal planning procedures – as well as the special inputs needed.

To be able to work effectively with women's rights as human rights, increased awareness is needed among all personnel and consultants. To achieve this, the donor agency will require an adequate knowledge base obtained through keeping abreast of research internationally. It will also require that all personnel/consultants have an adequate knowledge of the CEDAW. Sensitization on the issue of women's rights as human rights and its importance for development cooperation, as well as information on the specific Women's Convention, should be spread throughout the agency. This can be achieved through, for example, its incorporation into training programmes as well as through special publications and reading lists.

An adequate context-specific knowledge base for the countries in which the agency works will be essential for efforts to sensitize and secure the commitment of all personnel/consultants, and to ensure the development of relevant methodologies/strategies in the different contexts. This will require efforts to keep abreast of research, collect disaggregated statistics, and commission research in neglected areas. It also requires establishing links with existing networks and/or supporting development of new networks.

One important tool could be to commission profiles on the status of women's rights as human rights at the national level for all countries where agencies have programmes of cooperation. These could be made by local human rights organizations/researchers and would provide the necessary information to stimulate dialogue between the donor agencies and partner countries.

Even if all personnel and consultants working in an organization are aware of the need to work with women's rights as human rights in the context of their normal work, little will be achieved if they are not helped beyond the level of awareness to the level of action. This requires that the organization develop methodology and strategy and make concrete recommendations for action.

The most effective means of developing competence is through training (i.e., training programmes which are not simply providing information through lectures but which require the participants to make active contributions in terms of linking the issues to the work with which they are currently involved). If the organization has a gender training programme, the issue of women's rights as human rights could be integrated successfully into the existing programmes – especially if the organization has an overall 'equity' focus. In addition, special shorter courses on the specific issue could be arranged which include both sensitization and methodology development. The profiles mentioned above would also be useful tools for developing capacity.

The types of methodologies and tools developed will be dependent on the overall methodological approach of the organization. In terms of methodology the most important issue is to avoid development of complicated separate routines. The objective must be to change attitudes and clarify the entry points existing in normal planning processes and routines so that the perspective can be incorporated as part of the normal work of all actors. The most obvious entry point is at the preparation stage of inputs. However, impact can be made on programmes which have been underway for some time – through normal monitoring inputs or through special studies which provide the necessary information for promoting changes in the inputs.

When organizations begin working with a gender perspective, there is normally a cry for checklists. Adequate checklists are very difficult to develop since they cannot be as context-specific as would be desired. There is also a risk that – because of rigidity – they detract from the process of awareness-raising and competence development. Case studies are another popular tool, recommended in many contexts. However, the objectives for developing case studies have often been very unclear. As instruments for sensitization processes, or for in-training programmes, they can be useful.

Some form of guidelines could be usefully developed in different areas. However, development of adequate guidelines – which provide necessary guidance without becoming too rigid – is difficult, and can usually only be done satisfactorily when there is a certain amount of experience upon which to draw.

It is important to develop adequate routines for monitoring. This includes development of indicators which can be used to measure progress. Efforts in this area are not easy since monitoring, as a process, is relatively underdeveloped. This is one area where increased exchange could be very useful. Human rights activists and research groups/institutions should be able to give guidelines as to the best indicators of progress, and how these can be used in dialogue between the donors and their partners.

Concrete Action: What Can Be Done in the Context of Development Cooperation?

Donor organizations are less directly involved, and thus are dependent on the work of human rights organizations/research institutions, in actual efforts to broaden the concept of 'first generation' human rights (as included in the 1948 Universal Declaration of Human Rights). Donors can, and should, actively support this process in human rights organizations as appropriate – at national, regional and international levels. This will require that donors keep abreast of developments within this area through contacts with human rights organizations.

Donor organizations already play a role in supporting work in the area of the specific convention for women's rights (Convention of the Elimination of All Forms of Discrimination Against Women, 1979). However, there is still much more to be done. Both within the donor organizations themselves and within the partner countries, knowledge of the CEDAW is extremely inadequate. An important donor input could be information dissemination. In situations where the convention is known (and perhaps ratified) but not adhered to, donors could be more proactive by including reference to the convention and the lack of compliance in their dialogues with their partner countries.

They can support efforts to spread information and pressure for ratification of and adherence to the principles at international, regional and national levels. This means providing support for documentation, dissemination, networks and research.

Increasingly, donor agencies tend to prefer to work nationally with groups/institutions at different levels within the countries where they have programmes of development cooperation. This results in some countries having access to considerable support and others to very little. This problem has also been recognized by the OECD/DAC WID Expert Group on Women in Development.

In development cooperation programmes, there is increasing support for the development of civil and political rights – through support to development of democratic processes, new constitutions, legislation, judicial systems, police services, public administration, etc. This is an area of support which is, today, still extremely gender-blind. Even in organizations which pride themselves on their human rights profile, most efforts for women's rights are in terms of special separate inputs for women. There are very few efforts made to incorporate women's roles/needs/rights into existing support for human rights. This is despite the fact that the violation of women's rights has direct links to all these areas.

That there is still much to be done can be illustrated by the following examples. In organizations today one can find studies carried out on the transition to multi-party systems which have no gender perspective at all; support extended to elections where the inputs and resulting documentation does not include any information on women's participation – despite the fact that the statistics collected are probably disaggregated in collection; and programmes of support to trade unions which do not take into account the roles/needs/rights of women workers.

Support is given to development of statistics in programmes which do not promote desegregation and development of methodologies to achieve this end; support to development of the civil administration and to professional bodies such as chambers of commerce, etc., without taking into account women's roles/needs/rights; and support to media development which does not take into consideration aspects such as women's access to information channels, or the image of women portrayed in the media.

One can find programmes of training/education inputs in the area of human rights for judges and police which do not give attention to the problem of women's rights. The same programmes, however, may contain a component of education for women on their rights. The impact of such programmes will be limited in terms of improving women's situation if only women get access to education on women's rights.

Support is also given to constitutional development without adequate consideration of women. An example is given in Ashworth (1992) of the 1980 constitution agreed upon for Zimbabwe which gave women the status of minors, despite the fact that the constitution was developed mid-way through the UN Decade for Women.

There is also a role for donors in the area of humanitarian and emergency support. For example in support to refugees, more consideration could be given to who the refugees are and what conditions they face. As pointed out in Bunch (1992), conditions for women are at times intolerable, with blatant violation of their basic rights. Priority should be given to the development of methodology for incorporating a gender perspective into these types of support.

The greater part of donor engagement is, and will continue to be, in the context of the 'second generation' rights or socio-economic/cultural rights – the rights to food, shelter, health care and employment, etc. Considerable efforts have already been made in many agencies to incorporate a gender perspective into support programmes in all these areas, but without particular emphasis on the aspect of rights.

Most agencies today emphasize the importance of participation, especially in the context of 'good governance'. Tools are being developed to assist in the process of developing adequate methodology and thus ensuring adequate knowledge bases, for example Participatory Rural Appraisals (PRAs). The gender perspective is, however, still under-developed in PRAs. Many donors today stress 'village-level planning' and 'community management' in their rural development programmes, and in sector programmes in the areas of agriculture, forestry and water/sanitation. There is a great deal of rhetoric on the subject but little concrete experience. There is not enough knowledge of decision-making processes, both formal and informal, for such a process to be successfully implemented. Here again, the gender perspective has been neglected with the result that women's roles/needs/rights are not given adequate attention. There is a need for a great deal of research at all levels, but in particular at the grass-roots, on gender relations and women's political participation at the community level. (See Holm-Andersson, 1992, for an example of such research in Tanzania.)

Donors are giving increasing attention to special focuses such as poverty and social policy in relation to socio-economic and cultural rights. A gender perspective will not be included automatically. Efforts have to be made to ensure that the analysis and methodologies developed have potential in relation to gender.

However, recognition of the human rights aspect is increasing in the contexts of different sector programmes. For example, in the health sector there are several areas where human rights aspects are important, and where donors should be increasingly aware of the human rights aspects of women's involvement. Firstly, there is an increasing focus on access to health care as a basic human right. The fact that women have less access to existing basic health care services, less access to specialist services, and that their basic needs for adequate care for reproductive health are not met, must be treated as a human rights issue. This was stated clearly in the resolutions from the WHO Technical Discussions on Women, Health and Development in May 1992.

In the area of reproductive health, the question of reproductive rights is being given more attention, in particular the aspect of 'choice' in relation to family size. The aspect of population is thus not seen simply from a demographic point of view but includes increased awareness of the need to understand the reproductive goals and behaviour of both women and men, as well as the need to empower both women and men to make informed choices.

The problem of the neglect of the girl child in many parts of the world is a human rights issue. Female children are discriminated against from before birth, and are denied adequate care during infancy, childhood and teenage years.

In relation to the increasing problem of teenage pregnancy, there is a basic right involved in terms of the right to resume schooling after the birth of the child. In many countries this is not the case. Girls are not taken back into educational institutions. Genital mutilation is another health problem which is increasingly being seen as a human rights problem. There are human rights aspects in respect to HIV/AIDS in terms of rights to adequate information and care, as well as the right to adequate protection.

All of the above problems should be treated as human rights problems in the context of the health sector, with implications for adequate health care planning. They should not be taken out of the health sector and treated separately, since this would detract from the possibilities for real change – in both attitudes and practice.

Finally, it is important to note that it would not be correct strategy to collect all women's rights, such as those mentioned above, and support them under one 'umbrella fund'. Optimum impact will be achieved if women's rights are dealt with in the mainstream context, i.e., women's rights in relation to health should be dealt with by the health sector unit, women's economic rights by the economists, women's access to land by those responsible for land tenure issues. This is necessary to ensure that women's rights are not marginalized, and to ensure that there is potential for recognizing women's rights as human rights. There is also a need to ensure that aspects of women's rights are integrated into all the 'special issues' programmes developing in donor cooperation programmes, such as population, HIV/AIDS, environment, culture, etc.

Conditionality – requiring adherence to the principles of the conventions as a condition for continued support – will be difficult as long as there is inadequate information on the principles of the conventions. This applies as much to the donor organizations as to the partner countries. Most donor organizations have not yet reached the stage in their sensitization process where they have incorporated and internalized the principles to the extent that they can effectively utilize the conventions in dialogue.

Bunch (1991) points out that no governments determine their policies towards other countries on the basis of their treatment of women, even when some aid and trade decisions are said to be based on a country's human rights record. Ashworth (1992) suggests the possibility of adopting a Code of Practice which could be attached to various agreements, including the Multi-Fibre Arrangement and the GATT, as well as bilateral investment.

However, it can be questioned whether conditionality is a good instrument. A lot more consideration needs to be given to the pros and cons. Existing dialogue mechanisms should instead be seen as very powerful tools. There could also be potential for positive conditionality, or the 'rewarding' of advances in terms of recognizing and securing women's rights. Ashworth (1992) takes up the possibility of debt-forgiveness conditionality (debt swaps – such as those suggested in connection with the environment) and redirection of military expenditure.

Special attention needs to be given to the national machineries for women in development. Many of these organizations have been very dependent on support from outside donors. They have loosely defined mandates and very little concrete support from within their countries. Changes which have taken place in the past few years, especially in the political arena, have drastically affected the national machineries in many countries. Those national machineries which were closely associated with the political party have now been 'cut loose' and left to fend for themselves. While this can be positive in terms of increased independence, there are also negative impacts in the sense that the organizations lose all the financial support that they had from within the country and they often also lose their mandate to try to influence the mainstream from within. Many national machineries with this mandate experienced problems in developing adequate programmes to this end. However, some donors are developing an 'institution-building' approach with regard to support to national machineries in order to assist the taking on of this important mandate. When the national machineries no longer have this clear mandate, the donor support will also change.

Some national machineries have become non-governmental organizations, with all the problems entailed in terms of learning a new organizational structure, fundraising, etc. It is important that donors reassess their support to national machineries and find ways of supporting them in this transition period. Institution-building will certainly still be required, especially support for training in democratic processes since many of the national machineries were not run in a democratic manner. These organizations will require assistance to find new roles in a multi-party context.

It will also be important to investigate the ways in which these national machineries in their changed forms can assist in the process of envisioning women's rights as human rights. Most national machineries have had networks reaching down to the grassroots level – even if these have not always included all women, and have sometimes had negative images because of the lack of adequate action programmes. On the other hand, in some countries the lower-level branches of such national machineries were the most dynamic and had the most concrete action programmes. In efforts to promote women's rights, it will be important for donors to try, as much as possible, to support empowerment at the grassroots level. The grassroots networks of the national machineries have been under-utilized to date but there may be potential for utilizing them effectively in the future.

Inter-Agency Relationships: Some Concluding Remarks

Contact, cooperation, coordination and exchange will be increasingly important in efforts to envision women's rights as human rights, and to acknowledge this within the total context of development cooperation programmes.

The need for increased contacts between human rights activists/ researcher groups and donors has already been mentioned. There is also a need for increased contact between bilateral donors and multilateral agencies. This can be through direct contact or indirectly through foreign ministries or other ministries (for example, in the case of WHO, through the Ministries of Health and Social Welfare). Bilateral donors should follow developments closely with regard to policy, strategy and actions within the UN agencies in order to be able to support and press for positive changes. Support and pressure can be through comments on annual reports and plans, as well as briefing of delegates attending the annual meeting. For example, donors should be active in the coming years in following up on the WHO Technical Discussions on Women and Health (1992), where the aspect of women's health rights as basic health rights was stressed and the need for disaggregated data was emphasized. Donors can both pressure and support WHO in these efforts. Delegates to the annual meetings should be thoroughly briefed to be able to ask the right questions. Donors should also be involved in influencing UNDP to further develop a gender perspective in its work on social indicators, and in influencing the World Bank to include a gender perspective in its work on poverty and social policy.

There are UN agencies working in all the areas mentioned previously – for example, reproductive health, refugees, humanitarian assistance and population. Close cooperation should be developed with the relevant agencies. Donors also have varying degrees of contact with regional level agencies, for example, the regional banks and the SADCC. Even if the donor agency itself does not have direct contact it is possible to support and/or influence through the foreign ministries.

It would also be beneficial for bilateral donors to have more direct contact with organizations within their own countries working directly with human rights issues, both within government and in activist/research groups, and in particular those working with the CEDAW. It is important, too, to have contact with the financial institutions which work directly with the World Bank. Useful contacts could also be developed with regard to methodology with institutions working with disaggregated statistics.

There is a need for coordination of efforts and exchange and sharing of experiences. In particular, efforts to develop tools such as disaggregated statistics, networks, profiles on the status of women's rights and research could be usefully coordinated at national and regional levels. Donors could cooperate to produce common tools rather than expanding energies to produce similar tools separately.

Bilateral donor agencies differ greatly from each other and have differing potentials for working with the issue of women's rights. There are limits to the mandates and resources of WID/gender units which impact on the potential for promoting the strategies/actions proposed above. There is thus a need for increased exchange and support. The OECD/DAC WID Expert Group can, and does, play an important role in promoting cooperation, coordination and exchange between donor agencies. This group can also exert pressure on member countries. The issue of women's rights as human rights could be included, for example, in aid reviews as appropriate.

20

Legal Developments and Reform in the Inter-American System

LINDA J. POOLE

Multilateral organizations tend to operate within concentric sets of constraints which make advocacy administration a state-of-the-art process – and sometimes a guerrilla warfare operation to counterbalance organizational entropy and active resistance to change.

Almost all of the agencies in the inter-American system came into being prior to the major push for gender concerns; their internal policies are firmly entrenched in response to the external politics enunciated by their respective governing bodies. Many of the international agencies that operate in the region of Latin America are largely unknown and, within that grouping, the Inter-American Commission of Women (CIM) of the Organization of American States (OAS) is probably the best-kept secret. CIM works in the field of public policy reform. It is not a major funder of programmes, although it does fund certain types of activities to advance issues it feels to be of particular importance.

CIM was the first inter-governmental agency ever created to deal with women's issues. It was established in 1928 to pressure for suffrage rights because, at that time, only one member state of the organization had recognized women's right to vote. For years afterwards, the inter-American system raised no particular objection to the kinds of activities CIM was undertaking, mainly because they were very specific, related to basic rights issues, law and the elimination of discrimination.

However, in the 1970s and the 1980s, institutional and societal reaction to gender issues became a concern. Kathleen Staudt, in her book *Women, Foreign Assistance and Advocacy Administration*,[1] discusses the internal tensions resulting from a threatening perception of gender policies as entailing redistribution – reducing benefits from one group and giving them to another. Much of her discussion is particularly germane to multilateral organizations, perhaps even more so because they deal with multiple levels of actions and actors. I cannot resist one quote: 'Ideologies can certainly wreak havoc on organizational performance, and gender ideology is no exception.' This from a woman who has been an active proponent on the issue of gender advocacies!

Multilateral agencies, in particular, can provide a unique challenge to conflict management and foster consensus to forward women's concerns. They offer a forum to resolve the confrontations that may develop when state imperatives engage and interact with the concerns and demands of individuals. All agencies working in the region of Latin America and the Caribbean have specifically adopted policies to promote women. They are enunciated policies and they are adopted by their highest-level governing bodies. Nevertheless, as the Spanish adage says, between the word and the action there is a rather large ditch. Sadly, this continues to hold true with respect to gender issues in Latin America.

Accountability is an issue receiving particular consideration in my institution, as is the decision within the Commission of Women to situate the discourse of gender issues within the discourse of human rights and the strengthening of democratic institutions. If you take both of those issues and apply them as litmus tests to the range of activities we are working on, you will see that even institution-building can then be looked at from the vantage point of the issues of democratic process and strengthening of democratic institutions.

In particular, I refer to the national machineries for the advancement of women, which, in the public sector, are supposed to enunciate women's concerns and to achieve public policy change. To the extent that they are able to respond to the concerns of their constituencies, they represent an example of the democratic process and good governance. When the women's machineries are incapable of carrying out this role, either because they are under-resourced or because they are ineffective in responding to the concerns of their constituency, then the question can be raised as to whether or not the democratic process is being served.

There is one area where the multilateral agencies have a role to play and where there is a space for individual actors, international and national women's organizations and human rights groups to come together. This is the field of legal development, reform and empowerment, particularly with regard to national code reform. In Latin America and the Caribbean, most civil and family codes were reformed during the Decade of Women, but reforms to the penal and labour codes have not yet been addressed extensively. However, support and assistance to countries in the area of development of model legislation is emerging, particularly in the general area of violence against women; this could be of significance as countries can apply the appropriate results to their own realities. The process is already well-advanced in the CARICOM countries.

An additional focal point of this strategic area of intervention, which is now of particular concern at CIM, is the development of an inter-American convention on violence against women. A draft text has been prepared and governments are being consulted. This dovetails into an issue developing at the UN regarding whether or not countries are prepared to move towards something to complement the UN Convention on the Elimination of all Forms of Discrimination Against Women, or whether there is a decision to move forward on a declaration in its own right.

In my organization, the country delegates found that while the CEDAW is deemed to be an extremely important convention, it is, like most law, a product of its time; as such, it is a reflection of the values that characterized the society that produced it. When the UN convention was being debated, the issue of violence against women had not yet reached the international forum. Essentially this means that within the inter-American system, states have agreed to the process of developing an inter-American instrument. The OAS, with the support of its General Assembly, is moving forward with the consultation process on an international convention for the region. Situated within the context of international or inter-American human rights instruments, the body to which redress should be sought – at least as the text now stands – is clearly the Inter-American Commission on Human Rights.

When, in 1990, we first consulted women experts from across the region on what the commission could offer in this area, the women called for support for development of legislation at the national level and for an inter-American convention at the regional level. They urged that this convention be assigned the highest priority and the process started immediately because of the length of time required for consultation and approval – usually many years.

The convention also offers a unique opportunity for concerted action between non-governmental groups and the government, since each CIM delegate is responsible for the consultation process, for ushering the draft text through her government, and for forwarding the opinion of her government to CIM. This means that the CIM delegate is also a focal point for any interested group or individual on issues raised in the draft convention.

The CIM determined that the draft convention would be a public document, not private or limited in distribution. It is available to anybody who wishes to see it, as will be the opinions of governments.

Article One of the proposed Inter-American Convention on Violence Against Women gives an idea of the breadth of the document:

> For the purpose of this convention and without affecting the acts of aggression or injury qualified as crimes or civil wrongs in the domestic legislation of states, violence shall be understood to mean any act, omission or conduct by means of which physical, sexual or mental suffering is inflicted directly or indirectly through deceit, seduction, threat, harassment or coercion or any other means on any woman for the purpose or effect of intimidating, punishing or humiliating her or maintaining her in sex stereotyped roles or denying her human dignity, sexual self-determination, physical, mental and moral integrity or undermining the security of her person, her self-respect or her personality or diminishing her physical or mental capacities. Violence shall also be understood to encompass

any act or omission or conduct having the above purposes or effects whether or not it causes physical or mental injury or suffering.

This process was initiated by the women of Latin America and the Caribbean. We hope that it signifies a very valuable and mutually enriching opportunity for common cause among individuals, activists, advocacy groups, government officials and those who have state responsibility before the Commission.

NOTE

1   Kathleen Staudt (1985), Praeger Publishers, New York.

PART IV
Strategies and Action

21

Organizing for Women's Human Rights Globally

CHARLOTTE BUNCH

Many strategies have emerged in the last few years for linking women's rights to human rights. The political framework and context in which we make diverse strategies is important. For a vision of women's rights as human rights to succeed, women must be organized and a base of support built to articulate and demand these human rights at all levels – locally to globally.

Women are not just victims of human rights abuse but also actors who can define and defend human rights from the perspective of their own lives. Comprehensive definitions of women's human rights can then be drawn from women's perceptions of what is central to their basic integrity as human beings. From this starting point, women articulate and work for their human rights, not by asking existing human rights groups for their recognition or trying to twist women into existing human rights categories. Rather, we bring the insights and changes in consciousness experienced by women over the last 25 years into the human rights discourse in order to build a perception of what human rights means as viewed from the lives of women. This aspect of human rights has been missing from the largely male-defined concepts of what is central to humanity. Adding this dimension will strengthen the concept of human rights by expanding it to take greater account of the lives of the other half of the human race.

As part of this work, women need to use the human rights framework while also transforming it. Creative work towards that transformation has begun in terms of re-interpreting and changing laws. But women's political organizing is crucial to the success of legal strategies. Such organizing is also difficult to fund, because it doesn't necessarily take the form of projects or clearly delineated legal changes. Yet, any change in laws or policy will only be successful to the extent that women feel they have access to those instruments, and that seeking to implement them makes sense in their lives. The social, political, and economic capability to use legal channels is what makes laws meaningful to people.

Organizing and consciousness-raising in this area should enable women to define their own issues in a human rights' framework and learn what it can mean to see themselves as having such rights. On one level it is simple to say that women's rights are human rights. It seems so obvious. Yet, this connection is rarely made. It can therefore be very empowering for women to realize that their rights are not (or should not be) secondary but are fundamental human rights equal to other human rights concerns.

The recognition of women's basic human rights is also key to citizenship and women's full political participation in society.[1] One avenue for exploring the relationship between democratization and women's human rights comes from the UN slogan for the 1994 International Year of the Family: 'Building the smallest democracy at the heart of society.' The hypocrisy or idealism of that phrase is useful for addressing women's human rights. What would it actually mean to have democracy in the family? How is women's political participation in the public sphere (or lack thereof) linked to the lack of democracy and respect for human rights in the home? These connections were explored in the 1980s in Latin America and expressed in the slogan that emerged from women's participation in the movement against dictatorship in Chile: *democracia en el pais y en la casa* (democracy in the country and in the home). What happens in the private or personal arena is also political and has implications for the success of democracy and human rights in other areas.

While only a few countries such as Kuwait still deny women the vote, many women do not have effective political participation in society even where there is a formal democratic structure. Many of the constraints on women's citizenship are linked to the lack of democratic human rights in the family. In some countries women are legally denied the right to travel without permission of their male relatives (husbands, fathers, sons or brothers). Often women are prevented from exercising their right to free speech and assembly by male family members who obstruct their ability to attend public events or engage in political or civic activities. For example, a woman from one Amnesty International chapter in Africa pointed out that many husbands would not allow their wives to go out at night, which prevented their involvement in the chapter's meetings. Studies of why more women do not run for office in the West cite lack of family support or fear of abandonment by their spouses as factors that preclude their participation in this crucial exercise of democracy.

The Year of the Family can be used to examine the linkage between effective democracy and women's human rights. Both depend on women having access to political participation and the ability to enter the public arena where human rights are defined and defended. We must ask what it means to create this access for women in both directions: that is, to achieve democracy in the 'private' world as well as women's democratic participation in public space. It isn't just a matter of solving problems in the family and allowing women more power there so that they will be content to stay in the private sphere only. Rather, democracy in the home is part of what enables women to have the social, economic and political capability to exercise democracy in the public sphere where they can help to shape the policies that affect all of our lives daily.

Strategic Approaches to Women's Human Rights

In terms of specific strategies for incorporating women's rights as human rights, I will review where we are now on the four basic approaches outlined in my 1990 article.[2] I ended that essay with a schema of four approaches to making these changes and showed what their implications would be for bringing gender violence on to the human rights agenda. While these approaches are interconnected, they do have distinguishing characteristics which make it useful to review them separately.

1. THE WOMEN'S RIGHTS AS POLITICAL AND CIVIL RIGHTS APPROACH

This seeks to bring forth the gender dimensions of the most accepted human rights concepts, such as freedom of speech, freedom from torture, etc. This is the area where we have made the most progress because it is simpler to move on first. For example, the work of the Women's Project of Human Rights Watch described by Dorothy Thomas[3] links a feminist vision of human rights to these existing concepts and draws out their implications for women's rights. Thus they have broken ground in reporting from a human rights perspective on matters such as the state's failure to provide 'equal protection' to victims of domestic violence in Brazil or the sex discrimination inherent in many policies of the Polish government. Another example is the work of Amnesty International in highlighting women activists as victims of human rights abuse and reporting on the use of rape as a form of torture in state custody. Rape has also been acknowledged as a form of torture in similar circumstances by the UN Special Rapporteur on Torture.[4] Greater international attention is now focused on this fundamental female human rights abuse, but it has not yet led to recognition of rape as torture even when performed by non-state actors.

During the 1993 UN Conference on Human Rights, women are likely to see some progress in this area of recognizing gender-specific aspects of civil and political rights. The basic demand that women have put forward in the petition to the preparatory committee for the 1993 Human Rights Conference is to incorporate discussion of women in relation to all the conference proceedings and issues. Rather than the ghettoization of women's human rights, we seek an examination of the ways in which women are specifically affected by any human rights issue. For example, in discussions of political prisoners or racial discrimination, there needs to be attention to women's specific experiences where problems like sexual violence exacerbate their condition. Or we can look at how fear of violence curtails women's exercise of rights to freedom of speech and assembly.

Demonstrating the gender dimensions of issues that are already accepted as human rights opens the door to a broader understanding of all aspects of women's rights as human rights.

2. WOMEN'S RIGHTS AS SOCIO-ECONOMIC RIGHTS

This approach looks at the particular needs of women with regard to such areas as the right to development, health care, food, shelter and employment. These issues have been important in women's organizing for a long time, but they have rarely been articulated in terms of human rights. Work in this area is complicated by the lesser status given to socio-economic rights by many in the human rights field, especially in the West. Thus, although these rights are firmly embedded in the UN Universal Declaration of Human Rights, they are termed 'second generation' by many and often not included in what people think of as fundamental human rights. This problem has been exacerbated recently by the collapse of many socialist governments which did recognize such rights, and the tendency in the 'New World Order' to reject socio-economic rights as governmental responsibilities.

Women's rights advocates need to show how socio-economic rights are central to the achievement of women's rights. The separation of socio-economic from political and civil rights is clearly delineated in many international organizations and does not reflect the reality of women's lives where the violation of these rights is not so neatly separated. For example, take the case of a woman who is raped and then forced to marry her assailant and give birth to his child, as often happens to poor women in many countries. The numerous human rights abuses she suffers (from the initial sexual torture of rape to forced pregnancy, forced marriage and forced labour as his wife) result not from one area alone. They come from the intersection of the denial of her economic and health rights with the violation of her civil and political rights to live free from torture, to choose her own marriage partner, etc.

Women in poverty from Africa to North America speak of the impossibility of talking about freedom to exercise their civil and political rights and a life free from domestic violence without also challenging structural adjustment and other policies; these policies deny their rights to survival and leave them vulnerable to violent human rights abuse. Women fighting for recognition of their human rights advocate a holistic understanding of human rights as indivisible and interconnected. Socio-economic and political/civil rights should not be seen as competitive but as equally important needs that must be sought together, not one before the other.

3. THE ACHIEVEMENT OF WOMEN'S HUMAN RIGHTS THROUGH THE LAW

This is the third approach. The primary international legal instrument for women's human rights is the Convention on the Elimination of All Forms of Discrimination Against Women. Significantly, this treaty has not yet been ratified by many countries (including the US) and, when passed by others, has had more reservations attached to it than any other UN human rights convention. Another recent initiative from the Commission on the Status of Women is the Draft Declaration on Violence Against Women currently being considered by the UN. If passed, it will provide a stronger conceptual basis for inclusion of gender violence as a human rights issue, although as yet this declaration has no effective implementation mechanisms.

Nationally, women in all regions have initiated legal changes aimed at improving their human rights status; these are important steps but they are often not enforced effectively. In order for such legislation to be meaningful, we must also work for its implementation at every stage from the courtroom to police stations to hospitals to social welfare offices to women's homes. This requires programmes that train professionals working with women to understand and respect women's human rights, new laws that seek to uphold them, and educational programmes aimed at teaching women their rights and how to use laws to demand them.

Reinterpreting existing human rights treaties and instruments in the light of women's experiences is often as important as passing new measures. Particularly in situations where new laws on behalf of women cannot get passed in a given political climate, other accepted treaties can often be used to extend benefits to women. If a country will not sign the CEDAW, an argument can still be made that rape or domestic battery violate the 'cruel, inhuman or degrading treatment' clause of the UN Universal Declaration of Human Rights and, therefore, all governments have an obligation under that treaty to seek to end these human rights violations. There is a critical need to train more women in the international system in how to use existing treaties and bodies. An international human rights diplomatic training programme for women is called for: it would move around the world and give women access to such tools and information.

4. FEMINIST TRANSFORMATION OF HUMAN RIGHTS

This constitutes both a fourth approach and a perspective that can be applied to work in the three areas outlined above. This explicitly woman-centred approach is concerned with expanding current human rights thinking to take better account of women's lives. It begins with what women experience as violations of their humanity and then seeks to connect that to human rights discourse, rather than starting with pre-existing human rights concepts and trying to fit women into them. This transformative approach is the starting point for many feminists in claiming and defining women's human rights as inalienable. Beginning from this view that women have such rights, the question is not whether women's rights are human rights, but why they were excluded before and how to gain wider recognition and implementation of these rights now. For example, whether women have the human right to live free from sexual and domestic violence is not negotiable. Women have such a right. The issues are how to change the present situation so that it becomes more possible to live that way and what aspects of human rights' tradition and mechanisms can be useful to this endeavour.

The need for this transformation underlies much of the work in the other three areas as well. As one seeks to integrate women into the existing categories of a male-defined paradigm of human rights, the ways that women do not always fit and the need for expanding those concepts becomes clear. This transformative approach also empowers women to move away from seeing themselves as victims begging for rights to understanding themselves as agents taking action on their own under-standing of human rights. Thus women are not just asking for charity or social services as the most vulnerable, but are standing up for their human rights as citizens seeking to change the social order.

The International Campaign for Women's Human Rights: 1992–95

The strength of women's movements around the world is at the grassroots, and international strategies should build on that base. The power of women comes from the ways that we have learned to express our concerns and build movements that have grown generally unassisted and often totally opposed by governments and established NGOs. For example, violence against women has not been recognized as a major problem by most governments or funding agencies; it was not even on the agenda of the UN Decade for Women until the end of the decade in 1985. Since that time, women have put gender-based violence on the agenda from the bottom up all over the world, including several places within the United Nations where it is now being considered. This illustrates the power of women to bring concerns from the grassroots into the public arena even at the international level if we organize for effective political participation.

The Center for Women's Global Leadership has focused on gender-based violence against women as the issue which demonstrates most clearly and urgently what it means to expand human rights to incorporate women. Our work involves all four of the approaches outlined above but is rooted in recognition of the need to transform human rights from a feminist perspective. Our first Women's Global Leadership Institute in 1991, with grassroots activists from 20 countries, developed strategies for linking women's rights to human rights; these included the call for an international '16 Days of Activism Against Gender Violence' campaign. This annual campaign calls attention to violence against women as a human rights issue through local actions during the 16 days that link November 25 –

International Day Against Violence Against Women (declared by the first Feminist Encuentro for Latin America and the Caribbean in 1981) with December 10 – Human Rights Day. The 16 Days campaign has grown from an activity observed in about 25 countries in 1991 to over 50 countries in all regions in 1992.

Another strategy proposed by the Leadership Institute was the bringing of women's human rights on to the agenda of the United Nations World Conference on Human Rights to be held in Vienna in June 1993. Both the 16 Days Campaign and activity around the 1993 World Conference were seen as ways to go public with a vision of women's rights as human rights, and to work towards building a consensus in the international human rights community around these issues. A crucial part of building that consensus is organizing a base of women who understand that these are their human rights and decide it is important to demand them in this context.

During the 16 Days campaign in 1991, we initiated a worldwide petition to the UN preparatory committee for the 1993 conference, calling on it to 'comprehensively address women's human rights at every level of its proceedings' and demanding that gender violence 'be recognized as a violation of human rights requiring immediate action.'[5] By 10 December 1992, over 150,000 signatures to the petition from 115 countries had been delivered to the UN. The importance of the petition goes beyond the human rights conference: women have used it to initiate discussion at the local and national level about why women's rights are not already on the human rights agenda and what it would mean to include them. Women have translated the petition into local languages and brought the issue into the public sphere through various means, such as posters and local publications of their declarations on women's human rights, radio and television programmes, and visits to government officials to discuss what women want taken to the conference.

Since there have been constant rumours that the UN might cancel the conference, strategies for it have been devised that would be meaningful even if the conference never happened. We have sought to involve women in defining human rights for themselves and we have encouraged them to engage with local human rights groups on these issues. Through providing information about the conference and its regional planning meetings, we help them learn how to use international human rights concepts and mechanisms for expressing their concerns. Women in each region have prepared for their regional conferences by developing their own agendas, connecting women to existing human rights discussion. This has been frustrated by the continual shifting of the dates for these meetings, which makes it difficult for NGOs and women to participate as they have limited resources and time constraints.[6]

As a result of the petition campaign and work done for the regional conferences, it became clear that it was important to define and document women's human rights concerns in more detail. Therefore, during the second '16 Days of Activism Against Gender Violence', another phase of the campaign was initiated: local and regional hearings on the violation of women's human rights. Women have been holding hearings where testimony is given on both individual complaints and group cases of violations of women's human rights, as defined by women in the country itself. The records and documentation are being supplied to the UN Commission on Human Rights as well as to the Preparatory Committee for the Human Rights Conference. Women who could not hold hearings have also gathered information and submitted documentation on such violations.

Resolutions based on this material will be submitted to the Preparatory Committee and to the conference itself. In addition, an international hearing on the violation of women's human rights will be held in Vienna during the first week of the conference as part of the NGO parallel activity. Women from each region will present key issues from their context, and an overall set of international concerns will be presented to ensure that women's human rights questions are present even if they are not incorporated into the official UN conference agenda.

The public dialogue on women's human rights created around the 1993 conference should help build momentum on this issue; that momentum will continue through 1994 with the Year of the Family and World Population Conferences and into the 1995 UN World Social Summit and World Women's Conference. For 1994, the women's rights as human rights campaign will look at women's human rights and democracy in the family, as discussed earlier, as well as focus on women's reproductive rights as human rights in the World Population Conference debates. During 1995, the UN will celebrate its 50th anniversary with many events, including a World Summit on Social Issues early in the year and the next appraisal of women's rights at the World Women's Conference to be held in China in September. Since the last World Conference on Women in Nairobi, women have moved in the last ten years more towards establishing that women's issues are part of global agendas and must be incorporated there, rather than addressed separately. The World Social Summit and the World Women's conference provide opportunities to evaluate how women have progressed in advancing our perspectives on the public agendas of the day – around such issues as human rights, the environment, population and development.

One important example of what it means to incorporate women's perspectives in the area of human rights can be seen in the question of how human rights groups respond to religious fundamentalism which poses a major threat to women's rights. The various fundamentalists' attacks on women are in the forefront of the threats to human rights today. These fundamentalist trends are present in all major world religions – Christianity and Judaism as well as Islam, Hinduism, and Buddhism; strong factions in all of these are hostile to women's human rights. By denying the human rights of women, such fundamentalist movements are politically under-mining the human rights of all. The human rights community needs to understand this attack, not as a separate and difficult 'women's issue' but as crucial to the future of human rights. Thus they should defend women's rights as key elements in what human rights will look like in the next century. If the campaign for women's rights as human rights succeeds, women will move to the centre of defining and defending human rights in the next decade. Such a transformation should bring greater numbers, and strength as well as breadth, to the struggle for the human rights of all.

NOTES

1 '1994 International Year of the Family' pamphlet, United Nations Office at Vienna: Centre for Social Development and Humanitarian Affairs, Vienna 1991, cover and p. 34.
2 Charlotte Bunch, 'Women's Rights as Human Rights: Toward A Re-Vision of Human Rights,' *Human Rights Quarterly*, Vol. 12, No. 4 (November 1990), pp. 486–98.
3 Dorothy Thomas, in this book.
4 *Rape and Sexual Abuse: Torture and Ill Treatment of Women in Detention*, Amnesty International, New York, January 1992.
5 The petition, which was initially co-sponsored by the Center for Women's Global Leadership and the International Women's Tribune Centre, has been endorsed by over 150 women's organizations nationally and internationally.
6 As of December 1992, only the African regional conference had been held according to its original schedule; the others were postponed until January 1993, with even those dates insecure.

22

Preparing for the Millennium: Challenge and Change

Georgina Ashworth

The period 1993–95 is of intense importance in the securing of women's rights and autonomy within their homes, in their relations to the state, and on an international basis. We must grasp this opportunity to transform the current restricted understanding of human rights, which substantially excludes women's enjoyment of all rights and fundamental freedoms, and open women's access to the 'mainstream' human rights mechanisms.

With the current 're-democratization' of many countries of the world, both from internal social movements and pressures exerted by external powers, the securing of women's participation, representation and consent must be a priority, overriding the universal historic legacy of exclusion. Women must be ready to meet the accelerating challenges of the last years of this millennium.

I established CHANGE in 1979 as a women's human rights organization 'to advance the recognition of the inalienable human rights and dignity of women and to publicize their abuse, whether by state, commercial interest or individual.' This was before the Convention on the Elimination of All Forms of Discrimination Against Women named states, commercial interests and individuals as the violators.

It is sometimes quite hard to believe that CHANGE is an international non-governmental organization, because it is very tiny and has always been very poor. Yet it aspires to enable others to influence agendas, resolutions, and deliberations.

Since its inception, CHANGE has promoted women's rights through its activities and its publications, and has led a campaign for the ratification of the CEDAW and for the UN Decade for Women and the Forward-Looking Strategies in the United Kingdom.

For me, human rights constitute a philosophy of egalitarian human relations – engagement and compassion rather than exclusion or division, the equal value of human beings, and their equal dignity and rights to resources, personal and social self-determination and freedoms. This philosophy is backed up by internationally agreed standards and machineries which give us the practical means of securing those rights. To

150

me, feminists are human rights activists, just as important as Sakharov and his colleagues, and just as likely to be persecuted. But rarely will this persecution engender so public an outcry.

In the early 1980s, I struggled to put all this down on paper – what it really meant to me and what it should mean to the international community. I was using sociological and economics texts, and also the knowledge and language I had gained working in a human rights organization. That particular organization was headed by someone who did not think that rape could be a very bad experience, and its board members thought that human rights violations were always 'out there', never in their own offices, homes, or their home towns.

CHANGE believes that human rights principles must be included in gender awareness training and gender planning. Without that rights element, gender training often misses out on empowerment and the contentious area of political change. All aspects of human rights, including economic rights, need to be included. For example, the right not to starve has been undervalued in our very Malthusian 1980s and 1990s. If the right to a livelihood were really recognized, not sidelined into so-called third generation rights, it would change the concept of a state's obligations, the objectives and execution of public expenditure and such policies as structural adjustment programmes. It would even change electoral policies and we would have a greater sense of what economic democracy might look like.

Free market economics could almost be considered a fundamentalist religion. It combines secular Darwinism and a full-blooded sovereign god! However, beneath my own rhetoric there are rather more serious concerns. Governments violate women's rights to attract foreign investment. International companies violate women's human rights in the interests of profit and competition. Communities violate women's and girls' human rights where resources are scarce, and the female sex is not considered worth saving. At the very least, we need a code of practice to break down the apartheid of gender in the internationalization of labour. Trade is not as innocent as we are sometimes led to believe. In the push to export and to meet externally imposed targets in the process of adjustment, the first people to suffer are women.

Because the economic unit of analysis is the household, another expression for the family, this systematic deprivation and exploitation tends to be obscured or absorbed in cultural relativism. I think that we must, in the interests of women's human rights, do away with the household as the unit of measurement and with the anti-democratic concept of headship which, when used for men, means leadership and power, and, when used for women, means overwork. The household obscures the unequal division of power, time and rights, and it justifies the control of women by men as judge and executioner and all the violations that go on in the domestic arena.

Forced prostitution and trade in women must also be considered in terms of economic and political rights.

Another issue is humanitarian and refugee law, recognizing persecution on grounds of sex and gender and the appalling things that happen to women refugees even when they are protected by refugee and human rights institutions.

Democracy and good governance are key words being used these days by donor governments. We have to accept that no democracy is a good democracy when it comes to women, and no government is a good government when it comes to women. Accountability to women as a constituency is rarely considered. As a member of the UK democracy audit, I have a tremendous daily struggle to get my colleagues to redefine the democratic criteria and to include the issues of domestic democracy. Male violence in all its different forms is systemic and personal. As democracies tolerate the most amazing levels of violence against women, one has to construe that there is a useful control mechanism being exercised in the interests of the privilege of men. We need outcry and we need practical proposals for prevention and for solution. We need to move from victimization to imagination about how to change these acts of persecution and to prevent them.

Marriage, family law and reproductive and health rights are areas of great confusion in many countries, while in others they are major constitutional issues. All states retain power over women's biological and social reproduction, and in no country do women have the parliamentary representation to ensure that their interests in these most sensitive areas are promoted. We need to redouble our efforts in this area.

Funders must accept ideas at home, as well as 'out there', if human rights democracy and good governance is to be saved from becoming either a new form of colonial conquest or another flavour-of-the-year. Human rights constitute an underpinning philosophy, but practical measures are needed as well to transform practices and processes. Many areas need to addressed, from judicial processes and police activities to recognizing that economists can also violate human rights.

EDITOR'S NOTE

Georgina Ashworth recently wrote a paper on women and human rights for the OECD-DAC WID committee. See Appendix for recommendations in this paper.

23
The 1995 UN Conference on Women in Beijing

ARVONNE FRASER

The 1985 UN women's conference in Nairobi, Kenya, made history, proving to the world that there was indeed a global women's movement. The participation of over 15,000 women, a few men and 5,000 journalists conveyed a strong message to the world. In 1995 we must give the world a different message: that women are not just identifying and analysing their problems, but that they are seriously intent on sharing power and that they intend to be at least half the decision makers of the world by the year 2000.

This builds on the message that women's rights are human rights, and that the theory and practice of human rights is essential to democratic development. The worldwide women's movement, consisting of thousands of new women's groups organized during the UN Decade for Women (1976–85), has reconceptualized human rights, making it the basis for democracy and for eliminating discrimination against women through reforming law, policy and behaviour. Now, through the 1993 Human Rights Conference, the 1994 Population Conference and the UN Year of the Family, we are putting forward a new vision for the world: that women's participation is not only crucial to development but to democratization as well.

Conveying this new message and new vision will take resources – financial resources, time, and intellectual energy. It will also take strategic planning, beginning now, and we need to learn how to use political systems effectively, beginning with our own national systems. Women must undertake strong constituency building and use their power to make this a non-sexist as well as a non-racist world. We must build and maintain coalitions across political lines, understanding the tensions we shall have to deal with, and respecting the right to disagree on some matters while agreeing on our common agenda and moving it forward.

Some of us must work to become members of the official national delegations to the upcoming world conferences; others must concentrate on non-governmental activities, aiming to influence not just the conference delegates but world public opinion as well. All of us must learn to articulate the linkages between grassroots women, law, international human rights and democratization. For example, rights to inherit, have title to land, and obtain credit are not only crucial to rural women who need land to produce food for their families – gaining and using these rights is empowering for all women. Changing customs which deprive widows of all family property in many countries is only one of many steps implicitly mandated by the women's human rights treaty called the Convention on the Elimination of All Forms of Discrimination Against Women. This international treaty helps grassroots women, and it is women's groups in countries that have ratified the treaty who push for the legal changes in accordance with the treaty's mandates.

At the 1995 and preceding conferences, we must demonstrate how and where women's groups have pushed successfully for change. We must organize workshops, display the materials that have been published, report on research results and discuss strategies that work. We must illustrate our collective expertise. Though there is much yet to be done, progress breeds confidence. When women demonstrate their accomplishments, they gain credibility for all women.

When we think of the 1995 world conference, we must think in terms of the UN delegate conference and the non-governmental forum that traditionally precedes the UN conference. Whether it will be possible to hold a large, open NGO forum in China is yet to be discerned, so one of our strategies must be to understand and keep abreast of developments leading up to 1995. Traditionally, the NGO forums have been made out of whole cloth, been put together by an NGO planning committee that finds the hall or meeting place, organizes plenary sessions, and leaves the balance of the programme to be filled by enterprising women's groups and international networks who organize workshops, seminars, discussions and displays specifically for this forum.

It is not too early to begin preparations at local, national, regional and international levels. Plans must be made and funds must be sought. Local, national and regional conferences preceding the 1995 conference are important for building the momentum for a successful world conference.

Information about preparations for regional conferences and the world conference can be obtained from two international networks: IWRAW (the International Women's Rights Action Watch) and the International Women's Tribune Centre. Both will be publishing up-to-date information periodically on these conferences and how groups and individuals can be involved. The UN Non-Governmental Liaison Service is currently supporting the writing of a book on women's rights as human rights that will be published before the 1993 Human Rights Conference and will be useful for 1995. The Human Rights Centre in Geneva is now looking for ideas on the same topic from developing country groups. Women's groups must develop a process for deciding what they want out of the 1995 world conference and a means of conveying their ideas to government officials and to international organizations and networks.

Information is power and strategic planning is empowering. Begin planning now the kinds of workshops and seminars you want held at national, regional and international levels and what messages and strategies you want conveyed. Join with others, build coalitions to work towards 1995 and beyond. We must illustrate our power and authority for all the world to see so that by the year 2000 we will not be thinking and talking of government as 'them' but as 'us'. Certainly we will have defeats, but we will not be defeated. We must no longer be supplicants, asking for what we want. We must learn to exercise leadership and convince the world that our vision is a good vision for all. We know how to organize and articulate our concerns. Building constituencies simply involves passing on information, ideals, and ideas and urging others to join in the cause in which we believe so passionately. Putting the theory of human rights into practice – with women as full participants – is what democratization is all about. We must set about this task, and convert others to our cause, by using the 1995 world conference to convey our message.

We have made great progress during the last decade, but there is still much to be done at grassroots, national, regional and international levels. We can build on our progress and help create a better, less violent world only if we go forward with strategic plans for using every world conference between now and 1995 to fully gain human rights for women and take responsibility for implementing those rights from the grassroots to the international level.

Strategy for Linking Local, National and Regional Women's Rights Groups and Activists with Donors and Groups at International Level

Anne S. Walker, Australian-born director of the International Women's Tribune Centre in New York, rounded off the 'Linking Hands' conference by drawing the following diagram and explaining her strategy to link women's rights groups at different levels prior to the 1995 UN World Conference on Women. In the diagram, she tried to bring together some of the diverse elements that were discussed.

The left-hand column concentrates on local activities in cities, towns and villages. The double-headed arrows between each represent contacts, coalition-building and information exchange. The next column depicts activities at the national level by governments, national councils of women, national human rights groups and ministries of foreign affairs. The third column covers activities at the regional level – important in planning for the world conference as more women will have the chance to attend NGO Forums at the regional conferences than the world conference. The last column concentrates on the international level, which includes donors, NGOs, UN agencies, training and resources, and media networks. It should be noted that no one level is more important than the other: they are depicted as parallel, not pyramidical. Organizations on the right-hand side should try to supply support to those on the left. The arrows going directly from the local to the international level apply to individual projects which do not have to move through national and regional levels; however, project proposers do need to keep aware of what is happening at the national and regional levels.

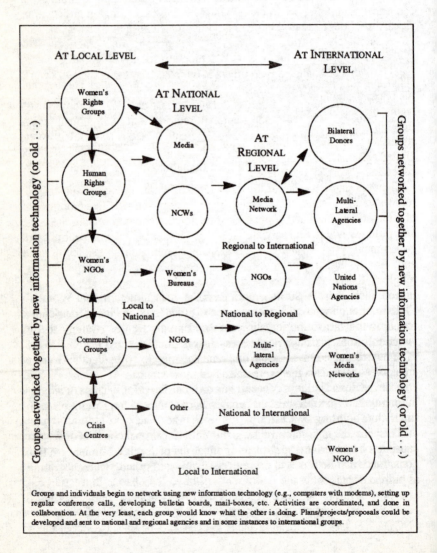

Groups and individuals begin to network using new information technology (e.g., computers with modems), setting up regular conference calls, developing bulletin boards, mail-boxes, etc. Activities are coordinated, and done in collaboration. At the very least, each group would know what the other is doing. Plans/projects/proposals could be developed and sent to national and regional agencies and in some instances to international groups.

24
Conclusion: Strategies for Action

JOANNA KERR

The preceding chapters have offered inspiring perspectives and approaches to achieving women's rights as human rights. The diverse country case studies indicate that women around the world all share various forms of subordination; the challenges yet to overcome are imposing. Throughout the book, the authors have articulated the inadequacy of the present human rights model to guarantee rights to women. In addition, mechanisms through which women can strive for change – aid conditionality, human rights laws, mainstream human rights organizations, 'development' policy, United Nations machinery, solidarity networks, women's groups or popular education – were all considered.

Genuine improvement of the daily lives of women requires substantial reform on many fronts. This entails the attainment and effective monitoring of international laws and conventions; the implementation of national laws and policies which support the rights of women; legal institutions and government systems which recognize women's human rights as legitimate; and, finally, the transformation of societal norms, be they cultural or religious, to give priority to the rights of women over oppressive customs. Indeed, there is still a tremendous amount of work to be done.

This final chapter tries to capture the essence of the discussions surrounding the various presentations at the 'Linking Hands' conference, on which this book is based. For two days participants debated the challenges to be overcome and strategies to implement. Naturally, divergent views and areas of consensus were expressed. The most significant conclusions to emerge are described here. They centre around five priority areas of action: international institutions, global conferences, national laws, religion and, finally, the community level.

This chapter also summarizes the debate that revolved around the capacity of bilateral and multilateral donor agencies, development institutions, foreign ministries and private foundations, to support women's rights as human rights.

International Institutions

There was unanimous agreement that international human rights organizations, laws, covenants and other instruments require reinterpretation or amendment if they are to promote and protect the rights of women. Various international legal scholars indicated that current human rights mechanisms clearly favour civil and political rights over social and economic rights. In addition, the mechanisms are, by definition, better able to protect the rights of men. It was suggested, therefore, that international human rights groups and instruments widen their mandate to honour the rights of women.

Irit Weiser, from the Canadian Department of Justice, claimed that we need to encourage treaty-monitoring bodies, such as the Human Rights Committee or the Committee Against Torture, to consider gender perspectives in the examination of their country reports. In this context, she added that it might also be useful to examine the overall relationship between the Human Rights Commission, the Commission on the Status of Women and the newly formed Commission on the Prevention of Crime. If the Human Rights Commission would consider the work of the Commission on the Status of Women, this would underline the fact that such issues fall within the human rights domain. Male-dominated human rights institutions, suggested lawyer Andrew Byrnes, 'could benefit from the participation of women who are sensitive to issues of gender for the protection of human rights.' He explained that this has not been the case because human rights bodies do not have well developed linkages with women's rights groups. If women's human rights violations are to be addressed by international bodies, these reforms must be encouraged by all parties – users, funders, member governments and, indeed, personnel.

In addition, international instruments explicitly intended to promote women's rights must be supported by all national governments. As Marsha Freeman explained, the Convention on the Elimination of All Forms of Discrimination is a legal and human rights document that is enforced through an inconsistent and underfunded reporting process of the CEDAW committee. If this is to become a viable instrument through which women can improve their daily lives, the enforcement mechanisms must be strengthened. That will require not only greater funding of the CEDAW committee, but greater pressure by donors and women's groups on governments to implement the convention's edict and to remove reservations made to it.

Without this kind of support, the CEDAW will continue to lack any authenticity. The South African government has used the signing of the CEDAW as sufficient acknowledgement of women without acting on its mandate. This has undermined transformation programmes initiated by South African women who want the CEDAW to be ratified by a non-racist democratic government.

It is also crucial that all international human rights laws and conventions be made accessible to women and legal workers in every country. Chilean lawyer Cecilia Medina recommended that the United Nations should disseminate more information about these international laws and conventions, 'so that precedents can be used to further the universalization of the scope and content of human rights.'

Global Conferences

There was considerable discussion about strategies for the forthcoming United Nations world conferences. Over the next three years, several major events are taking place which will require attention and input from women's rights activists and their supporters. The June 1993 UN conference on Human Rights in Vienna will be a crucial opportunity to address women's rights as a human rights concern. In 1994, the Year of the Family and the World Conference on Population and Development are potential platforms for progress on reproductive rights. These events, however, may constitute a significant threat to women's achievements if the agenda is influenced by religious fundamentalism, economic recession rhetoric or anti-feminist backlash which could institutionalize restrictive 'family policies'. In 1995 in Beijing, China, the Fourth World Conference on Women could be a catalyst to extract commitment from governments around the world to address women's rights as human rights, and advance the Forward Looking Strategies (the major document produced from the 1985 World Conference on Women in Nairobi, which gives recommendations to governments for the promotion of women's equality).

Some participants, such as Elizabeth Morris-Hughes, from the World Bank, disliked the scenario of endless global conferences which she described as 'just another example of how the men have run the business for the last 40 years.' Women are co-opted into this process and forced to deal with its consequences, instead of developing alternative methods of bringing about change. Moreover, as one African woman complained, the time spent finding money to travel to and attend these conferences is valuable time away from the real work of promoting women's rights at home.

Nonetheless, American lawyer Rhonda Copeland stressed that women are the most powerful constituency of all, demanding a broader concept of human rights and pressing for 'development' to include the fulfilment of social and economic rights. Women's contribution to any conference, therefore, will be profound, while benefiting the self-development of women themselves in the process.

It was evident that the lack of information regarding these numerous world conferences, their agendas, official delegations and preparations was causing considerable frustration. Arvonne Fraser urged participants to ask their foreign ministries for these details, and then to lobby chosen delegates to be accountable to women. She pointed out, '. . . that is the most influence that we have as individuals.'

Preparations were considered for the forthcoming United Nations conference on women to be held in 1995 in Beijing. Arvonne Fraser offered many suggestions on how to capitalize on this opportunity to institutionalize mechanisms that guarantee rights for women. Barbara Adams cautioned, however, that this meeting competes with the United Nations' 50th Anniversary – while women are seeking commitment from governments and media attention at the China conference, world attention will likely be focused on anniversary events in New York. Early and thorough preparations, numerous regional events and conscientious follow-up will be fundamental to achieving conference goals. Funding agencies were encouraged to assist women's groups in pre-conference activities.

One participant urged that the conference on women be used as an opportunity to 'build bridges with Chinese women,' many of whom are fighting with great bravery and creativity for their rights. As non-governmental organizations are forbidden in China, the state-owned All China Women's Federation is the only formal structure for women. Nonetheless, women are mobilizing independently and are seeking solidarity with activists as well as funding agencies outside China. These women can be contacted through international women's organizations and networks.

Law Reform

Reforming or eradicating the laws that deprive women of their rights has been identified as a crucial strategy by women activists throughout the world. By removing discriminating legislation or constructing laws that impart to women material benefit, women may gain the legal right to land, credit, employment or control over their own bodies. Florence Butegwa recounted an example in which women's groups in Zambia were able to mobilize women and men to lobby the government to amend the law of inheritance. This now allows a widow to inherit 50 per cent of the husband's property if he dies intestate, whereas in the past it was seized by relatives.

According to Elizabeth Morris-Hughes, the World Bank is currently providing assistance to African lawyers and activists involved in legal reform. Governance and human rights issues are beginning to be explored from a gender perspective. She explained that women's social and economic rights are not yet analysed within a legal context, though these rights have been emphasized within the Bank's investment programmes in education and health.

Progressive law reforms intended to protect women can, however, be rendered totally ineffective and irrelevant depending on the interpretation put on them. Human rights activist Tokunbo Ige stated that in Nigeria 'the whole court system is looked upon as a system which tears people apart as opposed to helping to actually solve problems.' She felt that women have to develop alternative methods of conflict resolution outside of legal structures, such as appealing to chiefs and leaders who could defend the women in their communities.

Nonetheless, Canadian lawyer Kathleen Mahoney noted that women's involvement in changing this 'interpretive arena' could benefit millions of women. In order to achieve this, more women should be appointed as judges. In addition, female lawyers throughout the world should be trained to develop legal tactics to challenge male-biased systems such as those in Brazil where the courts are using the defence of family honour to excuse the murder of women. The Canadian example of the Court Challenges Programme (described by Andrée Côté) is a useful model and one that funding agencies and governments should consider developing.

But this alone will not be sufficient, Shanthi Dairiam reminded participants. Mass mobilization at the national level to get these new interpretations accepted is still required.

Religion

The impact of religion and religious laws was ardently debated at the conference. Presentations by Women Living Under Muslim Laws representative Marie Aimée Hélie-Lucas and Rashida Patel, from Pakistan, provoked discussion on the use of Islamic law to subordinate women.

Hélie-Lucas told participants that interaction between women from different Muslim societies (the mandate of her organization) has shown that the notion of a uniform Muslim world is a misconception. It is imposed on women in order to make them accept the prevailing situation in their national or communal context. Ironically, according to the Koran, religious authority rule or hierarchy is forbidden. In spite of this, said one Sudanese participant, advisory councils of religious men which dictate oppressive laws against women in the name of the Koran are being created. Hélie-Lucas added, 'It is important for women to be able to distinguish between the cultural element in the oppression and the political use of forced religion and culture.' The rise in fundamentalism has inspired women's groups in all Islamic states to push, as one woman stated, 'for the eradication of Islamic rulers, not Islamic rule'.

With regard to strategies to free women from this religious subordination, it was suggested that an international conference should be held to explore a progressive interpretation of Islam; the participants would be Muslim scholars and activists from countries with various Islamic contexts, 'not academics from Oxford University'. When asked if the Koran did not inherently oppress women, Hélie-Lucas argued that all sacred texts, including the Bible, could be used to justify any custom. It was her recommendation that interpretations that respect the rights of women are acknowledged and promoted.

Several participants argued that Islam should not be condemned as the only religion that subjugates women. Christianity has several oppressive elements, including an increasingly popular morality based on traditional family values. Charlotte Bunch argued that 'when we call for a critique of fundamentalism we must be very clear that we mean the fundamentalism of all systems that have oppressed people. This includes international debt; debt forgiveness goes against the Protestant ethic and much of the capitalist machinery.'

Community Level

Many women's rights activists put a considerable amount of emphasis on reforming laws and institutions in order to have a greater, more all-encompassing impact on women around the world. Mila Visser't Hooft, from the Global Fund for Women, reminded participants, however, that the governments who implement these laws do not represent all women, nor do their laws enhance the lives of all women. She advocated increased financial support for groups which strive to change the sexist attitudes in their societies.

'Never underestimate national advocacy and working at the local level', Georgina Ashworth pointed out. Securing the political will of governments to perceive women's rights as human rights when their members have not internalized a value of equality is undeniably a huge challenge. Cecilia Medina maintained that the only way to counterbalance any inclination to ignore women as holders of human rights is for women to undertake actions themselves.

As Maria Suarez, who produces a feminist shortwave radio programme from Costa Rica, so powerfully stated,

> We are the ones that have our rights in our hands. We need to construct women's rights out of the daily lives of women . . . . When we talk about bringing international law home for us, this means to our bodies and to our houses where we have to deal with our men and our children.

She advocates popular education which can, through consciousness-raising, rebuild women's struggles and empower them.

At the local level, women's rights activists need to work with medical institutions, health systems, judiciary, and police officers. UNIFEM representative Roxanna Carrillo cited a UNIFEM project in Venezuela which trained police officers in how to deal with cases of sexual and domestic violence against women. These courses have become part of the core curriculum of the Venezuelan police academy. 'A very small number of dollars goes into this kind of project, but it has the potential of a multiplier effect.'

Donor and Development Agencies

Feminists have long documented the shortcomings of development programmes and policies that have yet done little to benefit women in the South. Scattered throughout the preceding chapters are recommendations to donor agencies on how best to support and promote the mechanisms that can guarantee rights for women. Carolyn Hannan-Andersson specifically addresses the key role donor and development agencies can and should play in the promotion of women's rights as human rights with respect to their own policies, programmes and funding recipients.

Shanthi Dairiam told participants that 'development' initiatives have failed because neither the balance of power between men and women has been altered nor male privilege dismantled. 'Development has been planned *for* women resulting in value-loaded forms of intervention which have accepted male superiority.'

Lourdes Sajor, from the Asian Women's Human Rights Council in the Philippines, pointed out to participants that the right to 'development' would seem to belong to a new generation of human rights. Yet, 'development' is often the cause of violations of women's human rights. 'Productivity, profits and progress, all tied to a world market economy, have brought with them the destruction of nature, the destruction of a way of life and the degradation of women.' If the right to development is to be promoted, new criteria and measurements should accompany this effort.

Chaloka Beyani, a Zambian lawyer, recommended that women's participation in both the design and implementation of development programmes should be a condition for donor lending. He also suggested that development agencies should base feasibility and evaluation of development programmes on criteria relating to standards enshrined in the CEDAW, as well as allocate funds to projects which are designed to promote or achieve certain aspects of the CEDAW.

Many participants discussed other areas of priority action for donors and development agencies. Marsha Freeman urged donors to put more money into research that examines gender relations and customary laws in countries of the South, and the ways that these can be transformed in order to emancipate women. Sudanese feminist lawyer Asma Abdel Haleem warned, however, that research is superfluous if it never helps its subjects. She quoted a woman from a village she visited, who asked her, 'Have you also come just to ask us how many children we have?' In the Sudan where 83 per cent of women are illiterate, infrastructural support to grassroots organizations is needed rather than research that often ends up on library shelves, said Haleem.

Canadian women's rights activist Nayyar Javed contended that many funding agencies are based in countries (and usually affiliated with governments) which are not favourable to women. If they are to take on the responsibility of genuinely advancing women's rights as human rights, these agencies should look inside their own structures and borders before hypocritically accusing foreign governments of mistreating women.

Shanthi Dairiam, from Malaysia, demanded space for and recognition of the need for women's collective voice in determining development goals for women. 'This would mean a constituency of women capable of recognizing what is in their interest and having the capacity to hold bureaucracies accountable for creating the conditions that will help them dismantle the structures of their subordination.' Many women echoed this sentiment, advising donors to strengthen existing women's organizations so that they can build a political force of women. Applying international legal instruments requires international top-down pressure; however, these endeavours need the underlying support of active and equipped women's groups.

Many participants raised the concern that this type of non-quantifiable output of human resource development does not fit with the funding criteria of most donor agencies. Norma Forde noted that donors 'like the other "D", which is documentation', thereby not financing organizations that are less able to develop proposals, evaluations and project reports. As a result, these organizations are often obliged to compromise ideals in order to secure external grants. Moreover, non-governmental organizations are forced to spend precious resources fulfilling these bureaucratic requirements. Suggested Mila Visser't Hooft:

> It would be really valuable if donor agencies could come up with one format of funding proposals. . . allowing us to focus on our work and not on interpreting policies, or searching for the right vocabulary that will fit within the donors' parameters.

Representatives from donor organizations admitted that funding mechanisms created obstacles for groups in the South seeking support. It was admitted that all donors have varied and complex funding mechanisms, but that to have one universal format would be unrealistic. Instead, groups should become familiar with these mechanisms, and approach field posts where applications to access funds are more flexible. She pointed out that donors are giving more attention to women's rights and violence against women, and that groups should take advantage of this.

Many participants agreed that changing international mechanisms, national laws or interpretations of religions required pressure from a strong international force of women. This global solidarity has to be established through networks, such as the Women Living Under Muslim Laws network. The traditional human rights community has sophisticated linkages; women's groups need the same. The crucial role that donors could play in financing these networks was made evident. Again, while the non-quantifiable product of a network usually disqualifies it from funding, several participants requested that donors take into consideration its integral purpose.

Ariane Brunet, from the International Centre of Human Rights and Democratic Development, emphasized that it was time for donors to take risks.

> It is paramount for our funding agencies to create an access fund for training women to gain accessibility to international structures – as well as to support women's networks. Smaller funders who have smaller budgets have a tendency to take bigger risks. We need to ask ourselves as funders why we are not willing to push our directors to take those risks. That is our fundamental responsibility if we believe in change.

Feminism is Global

Some issues surface in open dialogue among women's rights activists which rarely emerge in the written word. This book provides an opportunity to learn about the perspectives of women who are working within small organizations in the South, funding agencies in the North, and women's organizations in richer countries. Their perceptions about each other, interpretations of common strategies, as well as improved working relations are addressed in this chapter.

The donor–recipient relationship is inevitably contentious. Recipients are dependent on funders for their survival, while those who give money feel the pressure of accountability and therefore demand some form of assurance that their investment is used wisely. Funding can come with unreasonable conditions but, on the other hand, fund-seeking groups can make demands with little understanding of the bureaucracy that constrains project officers in dispersing funds.

Throughout the meeting, participants from women's organizations directed constructive criticism and some frustration at the donor representatives. If women's human rights are truly to be achieved, many participants agreed that the priorities, nature and beneficiaries of development aid have to be reconsidered.

Some donors were provoked to respond. The World Bank's Elizabeth Morris-Hughes asked participants to recognize that donor agencies have two important roles other than that of providing money:

> We have access to policy dialogue with national governments at the highest level. Second, we have the capacity to assist with very rigorous analysis and documentation – important for human rights and women's rights groups.

Mila Visser't Hooft insisted that participants challenge assumptions regarding donors:

> We have to get away from the concept of the 'other', so that we don't talk about the activists and the doers versus the supporters and the givers. Many donors see

themselves as activists – we should recognize that we are all in this together so we should all work together!

This profound statement stimulated several suggestions on how to build solidarity between donors and recipients. Adetoun Ilumoka, a Nigerian lawyer, noted:

> In the women's movement, there is no getting away from being an activist, even within donor organizations. I would like to appeal to our sympathetic friends within donor organizations to demonstrate their friendship by getting down to assist those with whom they work, to understand how they must manoeuvre within their system.

Akua Kuenyehia, from Ghana, suggested that donor agencies give recipients the opportunity to tell their own stories and to describe their own priorities. She stressed that there is a need for innovation regarding the process of funding in order to realize the aspirations of women. 'This is not in any way denying the tremendous amount of help that we have received from funding agencies . . . without that kind of help, we would not have been here.'

The conference title, 'Linking Hands . . . Around the World', suggested that donor organizations and women's groups, both from the South and North, should work together to promote women's rights as human rights. However, many southern participants expressed scepticism towards this 'global feminist' approach. Tesine Khan, from Pakistan, contended that global feminism is still Western feminism, and diverging perspectives must be recognized. 'Linking human rights to feminism' is premature in the context of her country, she said. Khan added:

> Other issues coming from the West include sustainability, good governance, democratization, and the environment . . . these are not the issues of concern to poor people in developing countries but rather how they are going to live from day to day.

Tokunbo Ige, from Nigeria, complained that northern-based international NGOs claim to represent southern groups when all groups are desperately seeking funding. She asked:

> Why should we link hands? Local NGOs cannot get support for their work so we have to affiliate with international NGOs. Then we all hold our hands up to the 'gates of heaven'. When the international NGOs arrive at the gates, they drop us and do the talking on our behalf.

Substantial responsibility therefore falls on women's organizations and activists in the North. Continuous dialogue should occur with southern women. Space for their voices to be heard should be created. Northern feminists can no longer see themselves as missionary feminists, nor force a Western agenda on to the struggles of women in the South. Adetoun Ilumoka stated, 'Women in the North must recognize how their activities and lifestyles affect women in the South – our lives are quite different.' In addition, alliances between northern and southern feminists need to put a priority on equal partnerships and this means giving more resources and control to southern groups.

Division among women is non-productive. However, differences can be appreciated. One of the most valuable characteristics of the women's movement is its eclecticism. Women of all types at all levels are struggling in a multitude of ways for various types of change. This diversity is their best weapon, because resistance cannot anticipate and counter each direction of attack. Solidarity which recognizes diversity can be built among women, but it cannot be assumed.

Finally, human rights promotion is ready for feminism. The human right to political participation, to vote, to economic independence, to health care and the mere right to survival is just as much the right of any woman. The time has come for women to take what is theirs by right.

BIBLIOGRAPHY

Agrell, J-O. (July 1992) 'Perception of Human Rights in Asian Societies'. Paper presented to the International Workshop on Democratization and Economic Development in Asia, Tokyo. Swedish International Development Agency.

Ashworth, G. (1992) 'Women and Human Rights'. Prepared as a background paper for the DAC Expert Group on Women in Development, Organization for Economic Cooperation and Development. Change, London.

Bunch, C. (1991) *Gender Violence: A Development and Human Rights Issue*. Centre for Women's Global Leadership, New Brunswick.

Canadian International Development Agency (June 1992) 'Background to Development – Human Rights and Canadian Aid Policy'.

Carrillo, R. (1991) *Violence Against Women: An Obstacle to Development*. Centre for Women's Global Leadership, New Brunswick.

Eisler, R. (1987) 'Human Rights: Towards an Integrated Theory for Action'. *Human Rights Quarterly*, 9, 1987.

Elson D. (1991) 'Male Bias in the Development Process: An Overview'. In D. Elson (ed.) *Male Bias in the Development Process*. Manchester University Press.

Fisher, R. (1983) 'Negotiating Power – Getting and Using Influence'. *American Behavioral Scientist*, Vol. 27, No. 2 (November/December).

Hannan-Andersson, C. (1992) 'Gender Planning Methodology'. Three papers on incorporating the gender approach in development cooperation programmes. University of Lund, Department of Social and Economic Geography, Lund, Sweden.

Hannan-Andersson, C. (1992) 'Experiences with Gender Training – How Did It Work and How Was It Used? Some Experience from the Swedish International Development Authority – SIDA'. SIDA, 1988–91, Stockholm.

Hannan-Andersson, C. (1992) 'Gender Aspects in Population'. Paper from a seminar organized by the Stockholm Group for Studies in Natural Resources Management on 'The Population Question as a Neglected Factor in Today's Debate on Natural Resources and the Environment'. University of Stockholm, 3 April 1991.

Holm Andersen, M. (1992) 'Women in Politics – A Case Study of Gender Relations and Women's Political Participation in Sukumaland, Tanzania'. Institute of Development and Planning, University of Aalborg, Aalborg, Denmark.

Human Rights Watch (1991). *Criminal Injustice: Violence Against Women in Brazil*. US.

Human Rights Watch (1992). *Double Jeopardy: Police Abuse of Women in Pakistan*. US.

Landry, Honourable M., Minister for External Relations and International Development (1992). Presented to the Annual General Meeting of the Canadian Council for International Development (May). Canadian International Development Agency.

Mosley, P. 'A Theory of Conditionality by International Finance Agencies'. Faculty of Development Economics and Policy, University of Manchester, unpublished.

Nelson, J. and Eglinton, S. (1992) *Encouraging Democracy – What Role for Conditioned Aid.* Overseas Development Council, Policy Paper No. 4 (April).

O'Neil, M. (1992) 'Men and Women Together', in Uner Kirdan (ed.),*Change: Threat or Opportunity for Human Progress* Vol. 4. UN–UNDP, New York.

Payne, J. (1991) 'Economic Assistance in Support of Democratization in Developing Countries: A Canadian Perspective'. Presented to the International Symposium on Democratization and Development (October), Canadian International Development Agency.

Plewes, B. and Stuart, R. (1991) 'Women and Development Revisited: The Case for a Gender and Development Approach'. In J. Swift and B. Tomlinson (eds), *Conflicts of Interest – Canada and the Third World.* Between the Lines.

Schuler, M. (1992) 'Violence Against Women: An International Perspective'. In Margaret Schuler (ed.), *Freedom From Violence. Women's Strategies From Around the World.* UNIFEM, New York, pp. 1–45.

Sen, A. K. (1990) 'Gender and Cooperative Conflicts'. In I. Tinker (ed.), *Persistent Inequalities.* Oxford University Press.

Staudt, K. (1985) *Women, Foreign Assistance and Advocacy Administration.* Praeger Publishers, New York.

Staudt, K. (1989) 'Gender Politics in Bureaucracy: Theoretical Issues in Comparative Perspective'. In K. Staudt (ed.), *Women, International Development, and Politics – the Bureaucratic Mire.* Temple University Press.

Susskind, L. and Cruikshank, J. (1987) *Breaking the Impasse: Consensual Approaches to Resolving Public Disputes.* The MIT-Harvard Public Disputes Program. Basic Books, New York.

United Nations (1979) 'The Convention on the Elimination of All Forms of Discrimination Against Women', General Assembly Resolution 34/180 of 18 (December).

APPENDIX

Women and Human Rights –
Recommendations

FROM 'WOMEN AND HUMAN RIGHTS',
A PAPER WRITTEN BY GEORGINA ASHWORTH FOR
THE OECD-DAC WID COMMITTEE IN 1992

Recommendations

Donors can contribute substantially to the eradication of violence and discrimination against women, and to the full enjoyment by women of their human rights and fundamental freedoms. They can work to overcome the gaps in policy coherence and in the application of indicators and method-ologies for assessing women's well-being. Recommendations on the methods of accomplishing these goals are grouped under Good Practice, Institution-building, and Conditionality and Policy Priorities. The cost benefits of measures to secure healthy, productive, peaceful societies through the promotion of women's human rights and the prevention of violence and discrimination should be persuasive, where moral arguments are insufficient. Gender relations are already regulated by states, through fiscal arrangements, social security, immigration law, marriage and family law, established religion and military service, and executed through all the statutory instruments, administrative procedures, and legal and judicial processes, as well as the executive and elective bodies. It is the duty of 'good governments' to enforce respect for women's human rights within them.

Good Practice

While donors are already working in the area of women and human rights, experience suggests that it is unlikely that all of them have full and/or widespread inter-departmental awareness of the CEDAW as an instrument of Human Rights, or of the gender dimensions to participation, good government and democracy. However, Australia has funded conferences in the Pacific region on the Convention and the Canadian government often takes the lead at UN Conferences in presenting resolutions based on the Convention or the Forward-Looking Strategies. Austria gives full support to implementation of the CEDAW. Norway reports:

Women are an important target in the efforts to promote democracy and human rights. . . In the revision of the Norwegian-WID strategy new emphasis is being placed on education, institution-building and legal literacy, as well as human rights in relation to women.

Denmark argues that:

the widest possible measures must be taken to avoid adverse effects of structural adjustment programmes on the living conditions of the poor and other vulnerable groups, e.g., women,

It also argues that short-term effects must be counterbalanced by adequate and timely external resources, otherwise they are unlikely to succeed. 'It may be difficult to reconcile progress towards democratization with the necessary rigours of structural adjustment.'

Amongst the reasons for this argument is that the continued use of the household (and the concept of 'headship') as the unit of economic and social research and planning, or of political analysis, is inefficient and unjust. Without gender analysis, which demonstrates access and control of resources (including time), there is no true picture of the society into which a programme or project is being introduced. It is damaging and inconsistent with human rights if a programme perpetuates, or increases, inequalities between the sexes, as many structural adjustment programmes have been proven to do (see, for example, *The Invisible Adjustment*, UNICEF ECLAC, 1986; *Engendering Adjustment*, Commonwealth Expert Group, 1989; *Women and Adjustment Policies in the Third World*, eds H. Afshar and C. Dennis, Macmillan 1992).

Hence, the incorporation of unpaid work into data bases (including the UNDP Human Development indicators) and into planning is essential to the effectiveness of project and programme assistance, since it presents better information on national and local economic activity and income distribution, and of the obstacles to the enjoyment of human rights (e.g., political participation, leisure, cultural and social activities), while subsistence production and marketing, properly recognized and supported, can be the backbone of national food security and distribution, improving family nutrition and women's livelihoods. In all societies women work longer hours than men, but the time and kinds of tasks involved are insufficiently recognized, (a) as an external subsidy to production and trade; (b) as services in themselves; (c) as management skills transferable into other economic occupations, thus depriving women of status and livelihood.

Departments, divisions or units for Human Rights established within Foreign Ministries or Development Agencies would increase their effectiveness and policy coherence if they actively included the CEDAW and the draft Convention on Violence Against Women, and the necessary reporting procedures within their remit. They should also actively include women's (international) organizations, groups and experts in consultations with human rights organizations, particularly in preparation for 1993

Human Rights Year, pre-meetings and debriefings on the UN Human Rights Commissions and Committees, and the Conference on Security and Economic Cooperation in Europe.

Similarly, development agencies and Foreign Ministries would increase their efficiency if they actively included women's (international) organizations, groups and experts in consultations on good government, democracy and participatory development, as well as economic reform, adjustment, and trade relations; also ensuring that their embassies and overseas missions are fully cognisant of the CEDAW, and use it as a frame of reference within their human rights reporting; that gender awareness training and gender planning includes a women's human rights component; that their own statistical gathering and use is gender-segregated throughout all sectors, country reporting, projects, and programmes; and that any census or statistical training for recipient countries also ensures this; that the household as a unit is not used, masculine terminology avoided except where applicable, and methodologies for the measurement of unpaid work are applied; that contractors and funding recipients have a proven knowledge of and commitment to the CEDAW.

Other measures which would ensure policy consistency include the engagement of more women consultants (and on equal conditions to male consultants);

- the adoption of participatory methods of appraisal, assessment, and evaluation, which specifically ensure the active participation of women;

- the active development of information and data bases on methods of prevention of violence and discrimination (e.g., through popular education programmes, social marketing, legislation, counselling) as well as the treatment of offenders (e.g., in law, sentencing, custody, counselling, aversion therapy) and of victims (police stations; law procedures shelters, social services; compensation; counselling) for application within different cultures and communities;

- the establishment of information and data bases on best practice and positive action in electoral systems, constitutional reform, political parties, administration, judicial training to eliminate the bias against women and the disincentives to women's participation in democratic institutions;

- the lifting of reservations they themselves have entered against the CEDAW and urged home departments to secure the application of the Convention within national law.

Participatory development methods have been evolved in many countries, often pioneered by women researchers (for example Joycelin Massiah at the Institute of Social and Economic Research, University of the

West Indies). Their essence is local, decentralized democracy, whereby communities are able to determine their own desires and needs, and responses to external development planning, and they are empowering and educational at the same time, respecting the individual and collective dignity of usually peripheral groups. Denmark assists Participatory Rural Appraisal, which

> involves people's participation in surveying their own locality and ranking their problems and needs. An essential goal . . . is to define the rights and responsibilities of the villagers and the project.

Institution-Building

Donors should ensure that their programmes of institution-building and training do not perpetuate or extend discriminatory practices in any area of technical assistance. Positive action is necessary to demonstrate that discriminatory practices are not transferred within projects or programmes. As stated in the DAC Principles for New Orientations in Technical Cooperation, technical programmes and personnel should not be involved in activities inconsistent with human rights.

With the still-pervasive exclusion of women from, and marginalization within, the political, judicial, administrative and executive branches of national and local government, serious efforts to ameliorate this situation are still in their infancy. In institution-building the following should be borne in mind:

- Banking services and agricultural or small-enterprise credit systems should avoid demanding husbands' signatures or excessive collateral conditions, ensure female staff are trained and promoted, investigate rural outreach services, promote small-scale savings and loans systems (e.g., the SEWA and WWF banks in India; upgrading of indigenous rotating credit/savings systems in Africa).

- Journalism and media training should ensure female staff are included and promoted in all areas of work, that 'news values' are examined to see where they distort, discriminate, stereotype or ignore women, and that derogatory images of women are not used to sell newspapers, videos, etc., violating their dignity or arousing hatred on grounds of sex; space is created for positive items about women's lives and economic contribution, as well as the barriers in their lives, which are more representative of reality; support for women's media (e.g., International Women's Feature Service, based in India; journals, newsletters etc., all over the world; action networks to highlight persecuted women).

- Constitutional, electoral, and law reform should ensure that women are 'written in' using the jurisprudence of the CEDAW, as well as best practice (including quotas, dual seats, party lists) securing the representative and active participation of women in all areas of political life and decision making, political parties, trades unions, and non-governmental organizations, avoiding the male-centred structures and procedures which are almost universal; law reform programmes are urgently needed to sort out the conflict between customary and colonial law, which prevails in many parts of Africa, in the interests of women's enjoyment of the spirit and letter of human rights law; ensure the burden of proof does not fall on the already disadvantaged; eliminate the reservations to the CEDAW (e.g., prohibition of women inheriting land in Kenya).

- Judicial training which guarantees non-discrimination and eliminates the biases noticeable in court behaviour towards female victims, witnesses, accused, jury members, lawyers, and in sentencing (for example, for first offences women are more likely than men to have a custodial sentence); the criminalization of unmarried pregnant females (for example in the Gulf States, Pakistan, Iraq) or of prostitutes rather than clients (Thailand, Kenya); non-prosecution of violent males, rapists etc.; ensure the burden of proof does not fall on the victim; incorporation of the CEDAW in jurisprudence.

- Police and security services training to ensure fair treatment of female victims, accused and witnesses (the victimization of women in police stations in India, for example, has been much documented, but also in Latin America and Africa); services for raped and battered women, female police and doctors/lawyers; restraints on male perpetrators, rather than connivance with them.

- Administrative procedures and training of civil servants, for national and local government and decentralization, guaranteeing equal opportunities and equal treatment, as required, for example, by the Australian government; close examination of bureaucratic procedures/delivery services to disadvantaged groups, and poor: accessibility, fair treatment, etc.; methodologies to use gender-segregated data for all areas of analysis, such as labour-market, unemployment, human resource, census, etc., surveys (e.g., use UN methodologies).

- Public sector training, ensuring promotion opportunities are egalitarian, delivery services are people-oriented, as above.

- Diplomacy and trade negotiations, also, especially need to be inducted into the acknowledgement of the human rights conventions, the Forward-Looking Strategies, and use of social (and environmental) impact statements (e.g., in the GATT) and UN and other methods of recognizing unpaid work as subsidy to production and trade (e.g., Acharya and Bennett in Nepal; Nuss in Bangladesh).

- Trades union training has often in the past favoured men only; good practice and materials encouraging women to take part in trades unions have been evolved in developing countries (for example from the Commonwealth Trades Union Council for the Caribbean and East Africa).

- Professional bodies, civic organizations, chambers of commerce and business societies, non-governmental advocacy groups, which make up civil society, have traditionally discriminated overtly and indirectly against women, and many still do: it would be a matter of urgency to ensure that these practices are abolished.

- Good Human Rights education would include the CEDAW, the newly developed Declaration (and Convention) on Violence Against Women, ensuring that the equal dignity and worth of each sex, guaranteed under the Human Rights instruments, receives full attention, as a deterrence to violent and degrading behaviours towards women.

Conditionality

There is only limited evidence that the treatment of women has ever been included in human rights conditionality for trade, aid, debt forgiveness, or diplomatic relations, in part because conditionality has only been considered where 'gross violations' of a narrow range of human rights has taken place. Members should expand their conditions to include knowledge and application of the CEDAW. Suppliers, contractors and consultants to development cooperation programmes should be required to prove awareness and commitment to the Convention and the Social and Economic Covenant, as well as to the methodologies ensuring the active participation of women in projects, as agents and beneficiaries. Non-governmental development, population and human rights organizations through which government funding is channelled should also be required to demonstrate this awareness. Proven gender-specific awareness of social and economic conditions in developing countries in which such suppliers, contractors and consultants would prevent the imposition of stereotypes with their negative impacts of programmes and projects; gender awareness and planning training, which includes a rights component, will avoid cultural relativism, and prevent the extension of discriminatory practices through technical assistance.

The adoption of a Code of Practice or Convention like the 'Sullivan Principles' or the European Community Code, which concerned the conditions of employment of expatriate commercial employers under the apartheid system in South Africa, would be a step to eradicate the 'apartheid of gender' and the exploitation of women through foreign investment and sub-contracting; this could be attached to various agreements, including the

Multi-Fibre Arrangement, the GATT, as well as bilateral investment; debt forgiveness conditionality (debt swaps etc.) and the redirection of military expenditures, could be means of ensuring that new funding goes into women's projects and programmes.

Policy Priorities

The proportion and type of donors – states' funding for women's participatory development – are heavily outweighed by 'mainstream' human rights and democratization programmes and projects, for which there is limited indication that women's human rights are taken into consideration (or gender analysis used); funding for women's organizations with a human rights perspective should be provided on the same basis (at home and overseas) as it is to 'normal' human rights organizations.

Technical assistance which (a) encourages the incorporation of the CEDAW in national legislation, local human rights jurisprudence and the administration of justice, as well as legislative processes, (b) overcomes the conflict of customary family law/colonial law, and (c) develops genuine protective legislation for women.

Programmes which are aimed at eradicating violence against women, including adoption of the Draft Declaration on Violence Against Women (and in the Americas the draft Convention) as well as for treatment of offenders and of victims (see in particular A Manual for Practitioners of Domestic Violence issued for the UN Crime Prevention and Criminal Justice Branch with the cooperation of the Canadian Department of Justice and the Helsinki Institute for Crime Prevention and Control; the Commonwealth issued a useful manual Confronting Violence which contains programmes for this prevention, through media and other campaigns, as well as the treatment of victims and perpetrators).

Women as a social group have as yet no legitimate forum for political self-expression; women's consent to policy is assumed without any consultative mechanism, although governments frequently work against women's interests, particularly in international negotiations (e.g., for foreign direct investment), and economic role stereotyping takes place, underestimating the contribution of women to the economy. Hence, donors should encourage the institution-building of independent women's centres and groups in order to ensure that, as members of civil society, they can monitor the respect for women's human rights, implementation of the Forward-Looking Strategies and the CEDAW, particularly with the approach of the 1995 World Conference to Review Implementation of the FLS, and enable women to build their individual and collective capacity to participate on a basis of parity with men in all national institutions, and to ensure equality, which is 'the (legal and institutional) capacity of women and men to mobilize domestic, community, national and international resources on an equal basis.' Thus documentation centres are required to build up knowledge of the situation of women in the country concerned and comparable information and strategies elsewhere; advocacy training to ensure women's interests are acknowledged and adopted into national policy; legal advice services such as those in Uganda which receive some assistance from the US and the Nordic countries; external networks for protection of independent women's groups and organizations, which are often persecuted (e.g., Turkey, Egypt, Pakistan, Kenya); local media, print material, videos etc., so that women may be informed of their rights (even when they are illiterate), and of their common experiences and needs (e.g., for women's police stations; changes in the law, for contraception; where delivery services are; that the statutory institutions are there to serve not rule them) without the male censorship so evident from any content analysis of mainstream media.

Donors could also finance a directory or data base of experienced women professionals to help with constitutional reconstruction; treaty monitoring; judicial and police training; conflict resolution; international prison-visiting teams; international refugee programmes/visits/reception/care; redirection of funds in order to implement many of the areas of institution-building and good practice detailed above; and funding for the participation and pro-grammatic cooperation of women's groups and organizations in the 1993 Human Rights Conference to ensure that these concerns are adopted by the governments.

INDEX